CO-AZU-417

SELECT TRANSLATIONS FROM OLD ENGLISH POETRY

BY

ALBERT S. COOK

AND

CHAUNCEY B. TINKER

REVISED EDITION

GORDIAN PRESS,
NEW YORK
1968

Originally Published 1902
Reprinted 1968

Library of Congress Catalog Card Number — 68-59036
Published by GORDIAN PRESS

PREFACE

THIS book is addressed to those intelligent students of English literature, whether under tutelage or beyond it, who have not been quite willing to accept the statement that Chaucer was the father of our literature and the creator of our language, and who have yet not been able to gratify their curiosity as to what might lie beyond, by reason of their inability to read the tongue of our pre-Chaucerian ancestors. We are persuaded that there are many who are quite aware that Beowulf was not the author of the poem which bears his name, who yet are uncertain how that poem compares in diction, in imagery, in character-painting, in variety of interest, and in loftiness of sentiment, with the *Iliad*, the *Æneid*, or *Paradise Lost*. We are convinced that there are those who are too well instructed to call Cædmon and Cynewulf *Seedmon* and *Sighneewolf* who still have no clear conception as to the relation, whether in bulk or character, borne by the extant poetry of the one to that of the other. We feel sure that there are those who would prefer to appraise for themselves the qualities of our oldest literature rather than remain in helpless dependence upon the dry or rhapsodical estimates of the current writers upon the subject. So long as there are educated persons misled into imagining the missionaries

and civilizers of Europe north of the Alps as mere
drunken savages or torpid churls, or into looking upon
them as fatalists and ascetics plunged in hopeless gloom
and continually occupied with images of the charnel-
house, so long there is need that convenient opportunity
be afforded to revise such opinions, and to frame juster
views concerning those ancient students of Latin and
Greek, those patriots who fought with Alfred, those
scholars who founded the empire of Charlemagne by
arts, as he by arms.

To this end their poetry should be rendered accessible. The prose can wait, if need be ; but specimens
of the better Old English poetry, translated, where that
is possible, rather than traduced, should be drawn from
the cabinets of professional scholars into the light of
day. He who will should have some opportunity to read
for pleasure that which may be well written ; to admire
what may be spirited, pathetic, or sublime ; to realize
the variety of theme and treatment within the four or
five hundred years which the period covers ; to compare
poem with poem, and, if possible, century with century,
or even writer with writer ; to trace the relation between
our older literature, broadly considered, and the later ;
and to do this unvexed, so far as may be, by mislead-
ing comment, while provided with brief suggestion on
important matters, and especially with respect to the
sources of fuller information.

By two things, at least, this poetry at its best is
characterized — by the sense of reality and the instinct of
reverence. The poet writes with his eye upon the
object, but it is with an eye that admires, that discerns

spiritual qualities and meanings, with the eye of the soul no less than that of the body.   Here is vivid apprehension, profoundly imaginative insight, worshipful awe, and sometimes a masterly restraint in expression.   Here is respect for simple manliness, admiration for magnanimity, homage for divine tenderness and self-sacrifice. The range is not small — from characterization of a lifeless object, like a bow, to that of the terrors of Doomsday and the music of archangels ; from the turmoil of ocean, which

> shouts aloud and groans in mighty pain,
> While sounds the tramp of floods along the shore,

to the colors of an imaginary peacock, the fragrance of a blossoming forest, and the splendor of sunrise over the sea.   To these poets heroic deeds are matters to be recounted with simplicity and sober enthusiasm, true kingship is sacred, the good things of life are to be duly enjoyed, the instinctive feelings of the breast before the mystery, the might, and the glory of nature are not to be restrained, while all is tempered by reflections upon an endless future and the due retributions attendant respectively upon evil conduct and right living.   Here are pictured, or reflected, men bearing their part of life's burdens, doing the world's work in stoutness or humbleness of heart, not without consciousness of an infinite background for the performance, and infinite rewards for high service, yet with senses alert to sight, and odor, and sound, to the spectacle of an old churl tangled and tripped by the ancient representative of John Barleycorn, the artistry of a beautiful book, the gleam of armor, or the thrill of harp-strings. They tell tales, drink the mead, race horses across the plain, ply bow and spear, are loyal to their lords, defiant of their foes, hungry for honor; moreover, when they see death approaching, they face it with solemnity — if pagans, with fortitude and calm resignation; if Christians, with godly fear and joyful hope. Not savages these, not mere drunken churls, not cravens continually occupied with images of the charnel-house, but men who challenge our respect, and deserve it. It is of their poetry that we would fain present some fragment in modern rendering as little unfit as may be.

Translated, where that is possible, rather than traduced — such has been our ideal, yet none can be more conscious than we how often the corruption of manuscripts, or textual problems as yet unsolved, or avoidable ignorance, or sheer incapacity and lack of literary feeling on the part of the translators — ourselves included — have obscured the qualities of the original, now by deficiency and now by excess. We are tempted to ask pardon of those who know; yet, on second thoughts, we ask rather for unsparing criticism in the form of better renderings of the same selections, or excellent versions of other pieces.

It will be seen that the book does not represent any particular theory of translation to the exclusion of others. Indeed, in view of the fact that opinions on the best medium for the translation of poetry are so divergent, the attempt has been made to exhibit a variety of media. Hence the latter range from prose to ballad measures, from blank verse to verse roughly imitative of the original movement. In certain cases, as in that of *Widsith*, the translation is nearly literal; elsewhere, as in that of *The Ruined City*, the rendering is decidedly paraphrastic. Thus the book should be useful as an illustration of the different methods of translating our older poetry, and at the same time point the way to something better than its own present form.

The best Old English poetry is, we believe, fairly represented here by specimens, while pieces like *Widsith* and the *Charms* have been admitted not so much for their poetic interest as for their bearing upon the history of culture. It was of course impossible to do more than make selections from the longer poems, but, when possible, an entire composition has been used. The desire to present complete productions must excuse the apparently undue prominence given to a poem like *The Phœnix.*

The classification of the poems is naturally unsatisfactory. A chronological arrangement was manifestly impossible; an arrangement by authors was equally impossible. The word 'lyric,' in the classification we have adopted, must be understood in its widest signification. The cross-references may in some instances aid in counteracting the faults of our arrangement, in addition to such value as they may otherwise have.

We take pleasure in acknowledging our indebtedness to various publishers, particularly to Messrs. Cassell & Co. for permission to use the extracts from Morley's *English Writers*, and to The Macmillan Co. for similar permission to use Tennyson's *Brunanburh;* the *Beowulf* selections are from the translation published by Newson & Co. (New York, 1902), and the *Christ* selections from

Whitman's translation (Boston, Ginn & Company, 1900).
The *Andreas* extracts are from Root's translation (*Yale
Studies in English* VII ; New York, Holt & Co., 1899),
and The Battle in the *Elene* from Lewis' *Beginnings of
English Literature* (Ginn & Company, 1899). *The Battle
of Maldon* was originally published in *Macmillan's Magazine* 55 371 ff. ; *The Wanderer* in the *Academy* 19 355 ;
A Love-Letter in the *Journal of Germanic Philology*
3 7 ff. ; Hallam Tennyson's *Song of Brunanburh* in the
Contemporary Review 28 920 ff.   The other renderings
appear here for the first time, and, with the exception of
The Dream of the Rood, have been made especially for
this book.

In the interest of uniformity, the editors have taken
minor liberties with the extracts as respects punctuation,
paragraph division, etc., and at times the spelling of a
word.   They are also, in general, responsible for the
headings of the various sections, and even for the division into sections of poems like *Judith* and *The Phœnix.*

The topics of the subject-index will, we trust, prove
suggestive to teachers and students, and may be pro-
ductive of entertainment to the general reader.

TABLE OF CONTENTS

TABLE OF CONTENTS

SELECT TRANSLATIONS FROM
OLD ENGLISH POETRY

I

EPIC AND HISTORICAL PIECES

WIDSITH

Widsith, the Far-traveler, designates the wandering minstrel who is here supposed to speak. The poem is of historic and legendary rather than æsthetic interest, nothwithstanding the poetic quality of one or two passages. The following divisions are recognized by Chambers in his edition (pp. 127–128): introduction (1–9); catalogue of kings (10–49); lay of Ealhhild (50–108); champions of Ermanaric (109–134); epilogue (135–143). Chambers' opinion concerning the date is (pp. 150–151): ' We have an exceedingly early poem, belonging probably to the seventh century, but reflecting the traditions of the fifth and sixth.' The senior editor's view is: *Widsith* may fairly be assigned to the latter part of Aldfrith's reign (685–705), or soon after. Under the influence of this learned and pious king, *Beowulf* may well have been composed; and the occurrence in *Widsith* of various proper names also found in the *Beowulf* would point to much the same date, if not to common authorship. Aldfrith's learning may have suggested lines 15–17 and 82–84, while the Picts, mentioned in line 79, would have been of special interest to a Northumbrian king who owed his throne to the death of his half-brother at their hands.

The edition by R. W. Chambers (Cambridge, 1912) contains an extensive commentary and copious notes, besides a critical prose translation.

Widsith unlocked his word-hoard; and then spake
He among men whose travel over earth
Was farthest through the tribes and through the folks;

3

Treasure to be remembered came to him
Often in hall.
Among the Myrgings, nobles gave him birth.
In his first journey he, with Ealhhild,
The pure peacemaker, sought the fierce king's home,
Eastward of Ongle, home of Eormanric,
The wrathful treaty-breaker.
Of many things then he began to speak:
10   'Much have I asked and learnt of men in rule
Over the peoples; every chief must live
Following others in his country's rule
By custom, who would thrive upon his throne.
Of such was Hwala, once most prosperous;
And Alexander, wealthiest of all
The race of man, and he throve most of those
Whom I have heard of, asking through the world.
  'Attila ruled the Huns; Eormanric
The Goths; over the Banings Becca ruled;
Over the Burgends Gifica. The Greeks
20 Were under Cæsar; Cælic ruled the Finns;
Hagena the Island tribes, and Henden Gloms;
Witta ruled Swæfs; the Hælsings Wada ruled,
Meaca the Myrgings; the Hundings, Mearcolf.
Theodric ruled the Franks; the Rondings Thyle,
Breoca the Brondings. Billing ruled the Werns;
Oswine the Eowas; over the Jutes Gefwulf;
Finn, son of Folcwald, ruled the Frisian race;
Sigehere ruled longest over the Sea-Danes;
Hnæf ruled the Hocings; Helm the Wulfings; Wald
30 The Woings; Wod the Thuringians; and Sæferth
The Scygs, and Ongentheow the Swedes; Sceafthere

The Ymbers; Sceafa the Lombards; and Hun
The Hætwers; Holen ruled over the Wrosns.
Hringwald the Herefaras' king was named.
  'Offa ruled Ongle; Alewih the Danes;
Of all these men he was the proudest, yet
He over Offa won no mastery,
But, earliest among men, while yet a child,
The greatest of the kingdoms Offa won.
None of his age won with his single sword   40
More lordship; he enlarged by Fifeldor
His bounds towards the Myrgings, and thenceforth
Angles and Swæfs were forced to be as one.
Hrothwulf and Hrothgar, uncle and nephew, held
Peace with each other longest after they
Cast out the race of Vikings, bowed the point
Of Ingeld's sword, hewed down at Heorot
The host of Heathobards.
  'Thus far I traveled through strange lands, and learnt 50
Of good and evil in the spacious world;
Parted from home-friends and dear kindred, far
The ways I followed. Therefore I can sing
And tell a tale, recount in the mead-hall
How men of high race gave rich gifts to me.
  'I was with Huns and Hreth-Goths, with the Swedes
And Geats, and with the South-Danes. I have seen
The Wenlas and the Wærnas, and have been
With the Vikings. And also I have been
Among the Gefthas and the Winedas   60
And Gefflegas; with Angles, and with Swæfs
And Ænenas; with Saxons and with Sycgs,
With Swordmen, with the Hrons, and with the Deans,

With Heathoræms and with Thuringians,
With Throwends, with Burgundians; there I had
A circlet given to me by Guthhere,
A welcome treasure for reward of song;
That was no tardy king! With Franks I was
And Frisians and Frumtings; with the Rugs,
And with the Gloms, and with the Rumwealhs;
70 So was I with Albuin in Italy;
He of all men was readiest of hand
In shaping praise, most liberal of heart
In sharing rings, bright collars, Eadwin's son.
    'And I was with the Serkings and the Serings,
And I was with the Greeks and with the Finns,
With Cæsar, master over joyous towns.
Wiolane I saw, and Wilna, and the realm
Of Wala; with the Scots I was, and Picts,
And with the Scrid-Finns, and the Lid-Vikings,
80 With Leons, Lombards, Hæthens, Hæreths, Hundings.
    'And I was also with the Israelites;
With the Ex-Syrings, Hebrews, Indians,
And with the Egyptians, Medes, and Persians,
And with the Myrgings; with the Mofdings then,
And once more with the Myrgings. Then I saw
The Amothings, East-Thuringians, and the Eols,
Istas, and Idumingas.
                              'And I was
With Eormanric, and all the while the king
Of Goths was good to me. Chief in his burgh,
90 A collar of six hundred sceats of gold
Counted in coin, he gave me — beaten gold;
Which I, home coming, in requital gave

To Eadgils, my protector and my friend;
For he, Prince of the Myrgings, gave to me
The land I hold, my father's heritage.
Then Ealhhild, Eadwin's daughter, noble queen,
Gave me another.   Over many lands
I have prolonged her praise, when my task was   100
To say in song where under Heaven I knew
The gold-wreathed queen most happy in her gifts.
    'When I and Skilling for our conquering lord
With clear voice raised the song, loud to the harp,
The sound was music; many a stately man,
Who well knew what was right, then said in words
That never had they heard a happier song.
    ' Thence throughout all the country of the Goths
I traveled; ever sought the best of ways,   110
Among the followers of Eormanric.
Hethca and Beadeca I sought; and sought
The Herelings, Emerca, Fridla; sought
The East-Goth, Unwen's father, wise and good;
Sought Secca, Becca, Theodric, Seafola;
Sought Heathoric, and Sifeca, and Hlithe,
And Incgentheow; and Eadwin too I sought,
And Elsa, Ægelmund, Hungar; and sought
Proud bands of the With-Myrgings; sought Wulfhere
And Wyrmhere.   Often was unceasing war
Where with hard sword the army of the Hræds   120
About the woods of Vistula must fight
For home against the folk of Attila.
Rædhere I sought, and Rondhere, Giselhere
And Rumstan, Withergield and Freotheric,
Wudga and Hama.   They were not the worst

Of friends, howe'er they be the last I name.
Full oft flew whining from that band the shaft,
The shrieking spear, against the cruel horde
Where Wudga, Hama, chiefs adorned with gold,
130 Sought vengeance for their warriors and their wives.
   'So have I ever found in journeying
That he is to the dwellers in a land
The dearest, to whom God gives, while he lives
Here upon earth, to hold rule over men.'
   Thus wandering, they who shape songs for men
Pass over many lands, and tell their need,
And speak their thanks, and ever, south or north,
Meet some one skilled in songs and free in gifts,
140 Who would be raised among his friends to fame,
And do brave deeds till light and life are gone;
He who has thus wrought himself praise shall have
A settled glory underneath the stars.

HENRY MORLEY

SELECTIONS FROM BEOWULF

The poem *Beowulf*, the oldest of the Germanic epics, is the most important relic of Old English literature. The handwriting of the unique manuscript in which it has been preserved appears to be of the late tenth century, but the poem itself is certainly much older. This is evident from the fact that one of the events of the story (the expedition of King Hygelac against the Hetwaras) is historical, and occurred about 515 A.D. Allowing time for the later events of the story, and for the growth of tradition and myth, it seems probable that the poem as we now have it is the work of the early eighth century.

All the events of the story take place in Denmark and southern Sweden. England is nowhere mentioned. It is therefore probable that some, at least, of the materials from which the story sprang had been brought together before the last migrations of the Angles to England. However, the poem undoubtedly assumed its final form on English soil, probably at the hands of a Northumbrian, who may well have been a learned ecclesiastic. There is some evidence in support of a conjecture that the influence of King Aldfrith of Northumbria (685–705) is perceptible in the poem (cf. Cook, 'The Possible Begetter of the Old English Beowulf and Widsith': *Trans. Conn. Acad. of Arts and Sciences* 25 281–346). Christian conceptions are to be found in every part; parallels to the *Æneid* occur here and there (Klaeber, in *Herrig's Archiv* 126 40–48, 339–359); and there are even passages which may be due to an acquaintance with Homer ('Possible Begetter,' pp. 329, 336–343; *Trans. Conn. Acad. of Arts and Sciences* 26 324–325; 27 398–406; 28 1–20).

An excellent edition of *Beowulf* is that by F. Klaeber (Boston, 1922).

9

The poem is commonly divided into three parts.   The first narrates the adventures of the hero Beowulf, who crosses the sea to fight with Grendel, an evil monster who has been preying upon the people of Hrothgar, king of the Danes.   The second part describes the hero's fight with Grendel's mother.   The third part describes how Beowulf, now king of his people, fights fifty years later with a fire-dragon, who keeps watch over a vast treasure-hoard.

The first of the following selections is from a kind of prolog which recounts the glories of the Danish kings, ancestors of Hrothgar.   Selections 2–4 are from the First Part; 5 from the Second; the rest from the Third.

1. THE SEA–BURIAL OF KING SCYLD

When at length the fated hour was come, Scyld, the valiant, departed unto the keeping of the Lord.   Then his dear companions bore him down to the ocean-flood, even as he himself had bidden them, while as yet the
30 friend of the Scyldings ruled them with his words and long did reign over them, dear prince of the land. There at the harbor stood a ship with curving prow, all icy, eager to depart — meet for a prince.   And in the ship's bosom, hard by the mast, they laid their dear lord, the giver of treasure, that famous hero.   Many treasures were there, abundance of ornaments brought from afar.   Never have I heard men tell of a ship more
40 splendidly laden with battle-weapons and war-harness, with swords and coats of mail.   Upon his breast lay many precious things which were to go far out with him into the realm of the waters.   Verily no fewer of their gifts and tribal treasures did this people bestow upon him than they who at his birth sent him forth alone

over the wave, babe as he was.   Moreover, they set up
a golden banner high o'er his head, and let the sea bear
him away, giving him over to the deep.   Sad at heart
were they, sorrowful in spirit.   No man can truly say 50
— no lord of hall, or hero under heaven — into whose
hands that burden fell.

2. THE SONG OF THE GLEEMAN IN HEOROT

There was heard the sound of the harp, the clear
song of the gleeman.   He spoke, who could recount 90
from of old the creation of men, told how the Almighty
made the earth, the fair-faced land, and the waters that
compass it about ; how, exultant in victory, He set the
sun and moon as lights to lighten the dwellers in the
land.   He adorned all the regions of the earth with leaf
and branch, and created life in everything that lives and
moves.

3. THE SWIMMING-MATCH

Unferth, the son of Ecglaf, who sat at the feet of
the lord of the Scyldings, spoke, and stirred up a 500
quarrel ; the coming of Beowulf, the brave seafarer,
vexed him sore, for he would not that any other man
under heaven should ever win more glories in this world
than he himself.   'Art thou that Beowulf who didst
strive with Breca on the broad sea, and didst contend
with him in swimming, when ye two, foolhardy, made
trial of the waves, and for a mad boast risked your
lives in the deep water?   None, friend or foe, could 510
turn you from the sorry venture when ye two swam

out upon the sea — but ye enfolded the ocean-streams with your arms, measured the sea-streets, buffeted the water with your hands, gliding over the deep.   The ocean was tossing with waves, a winter's sea.   Seven nights ye toiled in the power of the waters; and he overcame thee in the match, for he had the greater strength.   Then at morning-tide the sea cast him up on the coast of the Heathoræmas, whence he, beloved
520 of his people, went to his dear fatherland, the country of the Brondings, and his own fair city, where he was lord of a stronghold and of subjects and treasure.   Verily, the son of Beanstan made good all his boast against thee.   Wherefore, though thou hast ever been valiant in the rush of battle, I look for a grim fight, yea, and a worse issue for thee, if thou darest for the space of one night to abide near Grendel.'

Beowulf, son of Ecgtheow, spoke: 'Well! thou hast
530 said a deal about Breca in thy drunkenness, Unferth my friend, and hast talked much of his adventure.   The truth now I tell, that I had more sea-strength, more battling with the waves, than any man else.   We talked of this when boys, and boasted, being yet in the days of our youth, that we would venture our lives out at sea; and we performed it even so.   Naked in our hands we
540 held our hard swords as we swam, purposing to defend us against the whale-fishes.   He, nowise swifter on the flood, could not float far from me through the waves, nor would I part from him.   Thus we two were in the sea for the space of five nights, till the flood, the tossing waves, coldest of weathers, and darkening night drove us apart, and a fierce north wind beat down upon us —

rough were the waves.   The spirit of the sea-fishes was
roused; then my corslet, hard and hand-wrought, was 550
of help to me against the foes ; my woven armor, gold-
adorned, lay upon my breast.   An evil monster dragged
me to the bottom ; the grim foe held me fast in its
clutch; yet it was granted unto me to strike the creature with the point of my war-sword; the fierce struggle
carried off the mighty sea-beast by my hand.

'Thus did the evil creatures often press me hard, but,
as was meet, I served them well with my war-sword; 560
they had no joyous fill by eating me, wicked destroyers,
sitting round their feast nigh the bottom of the sea; but
in the morning, wounded by the sword, slain by the
dagger, they lay up along the sea-strand, so that they
could nevermore hinder seafarers on their course in the
deep channel.

'Light came from the east, the bright beacon of the
Lord; the waves were stilled, and I could descry the 570
sea-headlands, those wind-swept walls.   Wyrd often
saveth the warrior not doomed to die, if he be of good
courage.   However, it was granted unto me to slay nine
sea-beasts with the sword.   Never yet have I heard of
a more desperate nightly struggle under the vault of
heaven, nor of a man more sore beset among the ocean-
streams ; yet I escaped with my life from the clutch of
my foes, though spent with my adventure.   The sea,
the current of the flood, bore me on unto the land of the 580
Finns.

'Naught have I heard of like exploits on thy part,
naught of the terror of thy sword. Breca never yet, nay,
nor either of you, hath wrought so boldly in the play of

battle with blood-stained swords — I boast not much of that — though thou wast the slayer of thine own brethren, thy next of kin; for that thou shalt suffer
590 damnation in hell, good though thy wit may be.   I say unto thee truly, thou son of Ecglaf, that Grendel, the fell monster, had never wrought so many awful deeds against thy lord, this shame in Heorot, were thy mind and heart as fierce in battle as thou thyself sayest.   But he has found that he need not greatly fear the enmity, the dread attack, of thy people, the Victor-Scyldings. He takes forced pledges from you, he spares none of the Danish people, but he preys upon you for his pleas-
600 ure; he kills and feasts, and looks not for resistance from the Spear-Danes.   I, however, will show unto him ere long the strength and courage of the Geats in the fight.   Thereafter let him who may, go proudly to the mead-drinking when the morning-light of another day, the sun in ether clad, shines from the south over the children of men.'

4. BEOWULF'S FIGHT WITH GRENDEL

710   Then from the moorland, beneath the misty hillsides, came Grendel drawing near; and God's anger was on him.   The deadly foe was thinking to ensnare some man in that high hall.   On he strode beneath the clouds until he could see full well the wine-hall, the gilded house of men, all bright with gold.   This was not the first time that he had sought out Hrothgar's home, but never in all the days of his life, before or since, did he encounter among hall-thanes warriors more sturdy.   So

the creature, of all joys bereft, came roaming on unto 720
the hall.   The door, though fast in fire-hardened bands,
sprang open straightway, soon as he touched it with his
hands.   Thus, plotting evil, he burst open the entrance
to the hall, for he was swollen with rage.   Quickly thereafter the fiend was treading upon the bright-paved floor,
moving on in wrathful mood.   Out of his eyes started
a loathsome light, most like to flame.   He saw in the
hall many warriors, a kindred band together, a group of
clansmen all asleep ; and he laughed in his heart.   The 730
cursèd monster thought to take the life from each body
ere the day broke; for the hope of a plenteous feast
was come to him.   But it was not fated that he should
devour any more of the race of men after that night.

The mighty kinsman of Hygelac was watching to see
how the deadly foe would go about his swift attacks.
The monster thought not of tarrying, but suddenly, for
his first move, he seized upon a sleeping thane, rent him 740
in pieces unawares, bit into the flesh, drank the blood
from the veins, and swallowed him in huge pieces.   In
a moment he had devoured the whole corpse, even the
hands and feet.   He stepped on nearer, and seized with
his hands the great-hearted warrior on his bed.   The
fiend clutched at him with his claw, but Beowulf quickly
grasped it with deadly purpose, fastening upon the arm.
Straightway that master of evils discovered that never 750
in this world, in all the corners of the earth, had he met
in any man a mightier hand-grip.   But he could get
away never the faster for that.   He was eager to be
gone; he wished to flee away into the darkness, to
rejoin the horde of devils; he was not faring there

as in the former days.   Then the good kinsman of
Hygelac bethought him of his speech at even; he stood
760 upright and grappled him fast; his fingers cracked.   The
giant was making off.   The hero followed him close.
The monster was minded to fling loose, if he could, and
flee away thence to the fen-hollows; but he knew that
the strength of his arm was in the grasp of an angry
foe.   It was a dire journey that the destroyer had made
to Heorot.

Loud rang the lordly hall.   All the Danes dwelling
in that city, nobles and heroes every one, were struck
770 with terror.   Furious were both the maddened wrestlers.
The house reëchoed.   It was a great wonder that the
wine-hall withstood these battling foemen, that the fair
building fell not to the ground—save that all within and
without it was so firmly strengthened by iron bands, cunningly forged.   There, as I have heard men tell, many
a mead-bench, gold-adorned, started from its base where
the fierce ones were struggling.   The wise councilors of
the Scyldings had thought that none among men would
780 ever be able to wreck by force this goodly house, bedecked
with bones, nor to destroy it by craft, unless perchance
the fire's embrace should swallow it in smoke.

A noise arose, oft renewed; a ghastly terror fell on
all the North-Danes who from the wall heard the shrieking, heard God's enemy yelling out his horrid song, his
joyless chant — hell's captive howling o'er his wound.
He held him fast who in his strength was the mightiest
790 of men in the day of this life.

The defense of heroes would by no means let the
murderer escape alive — he counted his life of no avail

to any of the people.   There many a warrior of Beowulf's
drew his old sword; they thought to protect the life of
their lord, the great prince, if so they might.   They
knew not, those brave warriors, when they plunged into
the fight, thinking to hack the monster on every side 800
and take his life, that not the choicest blade on earth
nor battle-ax could graze that foul destroyer; for he had
banned weapons of war and every edged sword by a spell.
He was doomed to die a wretched death in the day of
this life; the outcast spirit must needs journey far away
into the power of fiends.   There he found, that foe to
God, who many a time ere now in mirthful mood had
wrought mischief against the children of men, that his 810
wound-proof body availed him not, for the valiant kinsman of Hygelac had got him by the hand.   Hateful to
each was the life of the other.   The evil beast endured
sore pain of body; upon his shoulder a gaping wound
appeared; the sinews sprang asunder, the flesh was rent
apart.   The glory of the fight was given unto Beowulf.
Grendel, sick to death, was doomed to flee thence and
seek out his joyless abode beneath the fen-banks.   Full 820
well he knew that the end of his life was come, the
appointed number of his days.   By that deadly fight
the desire of all the Danes was satisfied.

Thus he who came from far, wise and valiant in spirit,
had cleansed Hrothgar's hall and freed it from danger.
He rejoiced in the night's work, in his heroic deeds.
The lord of the Geats had made good his boast to the
East-Danes, for he had saved them out of all their afflic- 830
tion, the harrowing torment, no little sorrow, which
they had suffered and were doomed to bear in sad

necessity. A token of the fight was seen, when, beneath the spacious roof, the warrior flung down the hand and arm and shoulder — the whole limb and claw of Grendel.

5. HROTHGAR DESCRIBES THE HAUNT OF GRENDEL AND HIS DAM

'I have heard the people dwelling in my land, hall-rulers, say that they had often seen two such mighty stalkers of the marches, spirits of otherwhere, haunting 1350 the moors. One of them, as they could know full well, was like unto a woman; the other miscreated being, in the image of man — save that he was larger than any man — wandered in exile, and him in olden time the people named Grendel. They know not if ever he had a father among the spirits of darkness. They dwell in a hidden land amid wolf-haunted slopes and savage fen-paths, nigh the wind-swept cliffs where the mountain-stream falleth, 1360 shrouded in the mists of the headlands, its flood flowing underground. It is not far thence in measurement of miles that the mere lieth. Over it hang groves in hoary whiteness; a forest with fixed roots bendeth over the waters. There in the night-tide is a dread wonder seen — a fire on the flood! There is none of the children of men so wise that he knoweth the depths thereof. Although hard pressed by hounds, the heath-ranging stag, with mighty horns, may seek out that forest, driven 1370 from afar, yet sooner will he yield up life and breath upon the bank than hide his head within its waters. Cheerless is the place. Thence the surge riseth wan to the clouds, when the winds stir up foul weather till the air thicken and the heavens weep.

'Now once again help rests with thee alone. Thou knowest not yet the spot, the savage place where thou mayst find the sinful creature.'

6. A LAMENT

Many olden treasures were lying in that cave of earth where a certain man in days of yore had hidden away the dear possessions, taking thought for the great bequest of his noble kin. Death had snatched away those men in times gone by, and, at the last, the one who tarried longest there of all that mighty line was mourning for his friends; yet he would fain live, that he might enjoy for a little time those olden treasures.   2240

There was a new mound ready on the plain, near to the cliff hard by the ocean-waves, made fast by cunning craft. Thither the keeper of rings bore that heavy store of beaten gold, the princely treasures; and he spoke a few words: 'Now do thou hold, O Earth— since heroes could not hold—this princely treasure, for lo! in thee at first the good men found it. Every man of my people who hath yielded up this life, dread 2250 slaughter, death in war, hath swept away;—they had known the pleasures of the hall! None have I to wield the sword, none to burnish the plated beaker, the precious drinking-cup;—the warrior-heroes are departed otherwhere. The hard helmet, decked with gold, must be bereft of its adornments; they sleep who once did brighten it, they who prepared the masks of war.

Likewise the coat of mail which, amid the crash of shields,
was proof against the bite of swords in battle, molders
2260 with the hero; the byrnie may no longer make far
journeys with the war-leader, together with heroes.
There is no joy of harp, no mirth of the gleewood, no
good hawk swinging through the hall, no swift horse
beating with his hoof the castle-yard.   Baleful death
hath sent forth many mortals on their way.'   Thus,
alone and heavy-hearted, he sorrowfully lamented for
them all, mournfully weeping by day and night until the
surge of death touched at his heart.

7. THE PASSING OF BEOWULF

But the wound which the earth-dragon had given him
began to burn and swell; presently he found that poison,
deadly venom, was surging in his breast.   Then the
prince, still wise in mind, moved along so that he might
seat him by the mound;[1] he saw that work of giants,
saw how the rocky arches, standing firm on their pillars,
within upheld the earth-hall everlasting.   Then the
2720 thane[2] surpassing good, taking water, with his hands
bathed the great king, his own dear lord all gory and
wearied with battle, and loosened his helmet.

Beowulf spoke and uttered words, despite his wound,
his piteous battle-hurt; full well he knew that his life of
earthly joy was spent, that the appointed number of his
days was run, and death exceeding near: 'Now would
2730 I give my war-harness unto my son, had I been granted

---

[1] See above, *A Lament*, p. 19.
[2] **Wiglaf**, who fought with Beowulf against the dragon.

any heir born of my body to come after me. Fifty
winters have I ruled this people; yet there was never a
king of all the neighbor-tribes who durst attack me with
the sword, or oppress me with terror. In my home I
awaited what the times held in store for me, kept well
mine own, sought out no wily quarrels, swore not many a
false oath. In all this I can rejoice, though death-sick 2740
with my wounds, inasmuch as the Ruler of men cannot reproach me with murder of kinsmen, when my
life parteth from my body. Now do thou, dear Wiglaf,
lightly go and view the hoard beneath the gray rock, now
the dragon lieth low, sleepeth sore wounded, bereft of his
treasure. Do thou make haste that I may behold the
olden treasures, that store of gold, and look upon those
bright and curious gems; and thus, having seen the treasured wealth, I may the easier quit life and the kingdom 2750
which long I have ruled.'

And I have heard how the son of Weohstan after
these words quickly obeyed his wounded lord, sick from
the battle; he bore his ringed mail-shirt, the woven
battle-sark, beneath the roof of the cave. And the brave
thane, exultant victor, as he went by the seat, saw many
precious jewels, much glistering gold lying upon the
ground, and wondrous treasures on the wall, and the den
of the dragon, the old twilight-flier; bowls lay there, 2760
vessels of bygone men, with none to brighten them, their
adornments fallen away. There was many a helmet old
and rusty, many an arm-ring cunningly twisted. Treasure of gold found in the earth can easily puff with pride
the heart of any man, hide it who will. Likewise he
saw a banner all of gold standing there, high above the

hoard, greatest of wonders, woven by skill of hand; from
2770 it there shone a ray of light, so that he could see the
cavern-floor, and examine the fair jewels.   Naught was
to be seen of the dragon there, for the sword had undone
him!

Thus I have heard how one man alone at his own free
will plundered the hoard within the cave, the old work
of the giants, how he laid in his bosom beakers and
dishes; he took the banner, too, that brightest of beacons.
The old lord's blade, with its iron edge, had sorely injured
2780 him who long had been the owner of these treasures,
who at midnight had borne about the fiery terror, dread-
fully surging, hot before the hoard, until he died the
death.

The messenger was in haste, eager to return, enriched
with spoils.   The great-hearted man was spurred with
longing to know whether he would find alive the lord of
the Weders, albeit grievously sick, in the place where he
had left him.   And bringing the treasures, he found the
2790 great prince, his lord, bleeding, at the point of death; he
began to sprinkle him again with water, until the word's
point broke through the treasury of his heart and Beowulf spoke, aged and sorrowful, as he gazed upon the
gold : 'I utter thanks unto the Ruler of all, King of
glory, the everlasting Lord, for these fair things which
here I look upon, inasmuch as ere my death-day I have
been able to win them for my people.   I have sold and
2800 paid mine aged life for the treasure-hoard.   Fulfil ye
now the needs of the people.   Here can I be no more.
Bid the brave warriors rear a splendid mound at the sea-
cape after my body is burned.   There on Whale's Ness

shall it tower high as a memorial for my people, so that seafarers, they who drive from far their great ships over the misty floods, may in after-time call it " Beowulf's Mound." '

The great-hearted king took from his neck the ring of gold; gave to his thane, the youthful warrior, his 2810 helmet, gold-adorned, his ring and his byrnie, bade him enjoy them well: ' Thou art the latest left of all our kin, the Wægmundings. Wyrd hath swept away all my kinsmen, heroes in their might, to the appointed doom. I must after them.' That was the old king's last word from the thoughts of his heart, ere he yielded to the bale-fire, the hotly surging flames. His soul departed from out his bosom unto the reward of the righteous. 2820

8. THE FUNERAL PYRE

Then the Geatish people fashioned for him a mighty pile upon the ground, all hung with helms and war-shields and bright byrnies, even as he had entreated them ; and 3140 in the midst of it the sorrowing men laid their great king, their beloved lord.[1] Then the warriors began to kindle the greatest of funeral fires upon the mound. Uprose the wood-smoke, black above the flame; blazing fire roared, mingled with a sound of weeping when the tumult of the wind was stilled, until, hot within the breast, it had consumed the bony frame. Sad at heart, with care-laden soul, they mourned the fall of their lord.[2] . . . Heaven swallowed up the smoke.

[1] Note the points of likeness and difference between this and the sea-burial of Scyld, p. 10.   [2] MS. defective.

Then the Weder people made a mound upon the cliff, high and broad, to be seen afar of seafaring men ; and ₃₁₆₀ ten days they built it, the war-hero's beacon. They made a wall round about the ashes of the fire, even as the wisest of men could most worthily devise. Within the mound they put the rings and the jewels, all the adornments which the brave-hearted men had taken from the hoard ; they let the earth hold the treasure of heroes, hid the gold in the ground, where it still remains, as useless unto men as it was of yore.

₃₁₇₀   Then warriors, sons of princes, twelve in all, rode about the mound ; they had in mind to bewail their sorrow, mourn their king, utter the dirge, and speak of their hero ; they praised his courage, and greatly commended his mighty deeds. Thus it is fitting that a man should praise his lord in words and cherish him in heart when he must forth from the fleeting body.

So the Geatish people, companions of his hearth, ₃₁₈₀ mourned the fall of their lord; said that he was a mighty king, the mildest and kindest of men, most gracious to his people and most desirous of praise.

CHAUNCEY B. TINKER.

THE BATTLE OF BRUNANBURH

This poem is entered in the *Saxon Chronicle* under the year 937, as a historical document. Æthelstan, son of Edward the Elder, grandson of Alfred, was king of the West-Saxons and Mercians from 925 to 940, and became overlord of all England. His alliance with the Frankish kings, which he formed by the marriage of his sisters, made his name famous on the Continent. Gardiner says of him: ' Æthelstan's greatness drew upon him the jealousy of the king of the Scots and of all the northern kings. In 937 he defeated them all in a great battle at Brunanburh.' Brunanburh is identified by Oman with Birrenswark, the site of a Roman camp, some 920 feet above sea-level, and a couple of miles north of Carlyle's Ecclefechan.

Edmund succeeded King Æthelstan in 940. Anlaf was Olaf Sitricson, also known as Olaf Cuaran, who, with his father-in-law Constantine, probably led the Scots; for his connection with *Havelok the Dane*, see Wells' *Manual of the Writings in Middle English*, pp. 13–14. Constantine was Constantine III, who began to reign in 900. The fleet from Dublin was probably under Olaf Godfreyson. For all these, and Æthelstan (Athelstan), see the *Dictionary of National Biography*.

Compare Tennyson's note below, and that prefixed to the *Battle of Maldon*, p. 31; Hallam Tennyson's translation will be found in the Appendix, p. 178. The account of the battle should be compared with that in the *Judith*, from which it is evidently imitated.

TENNYSON'S NOTE. Constantinus, King of the Scots, after having sworn allegiance to Athelstan, allied himself with the Danes of Ireland under Anlaf, and invading England, was defeated by Athelstan and his brother Edmund with great slaughter at Brunanburh in the year 937.

I

[1] Athelstan King,
  Lord among Earls,
  Bracelet-bestower and
  Baron of Barons,
  He with his brother,
  Edmund Atheling,
  Gaining a lifelong
  Glory in battle,
  Slew with the sword-edge
  There by Brunanburh,
  Brake the shield-wall,
  Hewed the linden-wood,[2]
  Hacked the battle-shield,
Sons of Edward with hammered brands.

II

  Theirs was a greatness
  Got from their grandsires —
  Theirs that so often in
  Strife with their enemies
Struck for their hoards and their hearths and their
    homes.

III

10
  Bowed the spoiler,
  Bent the Scotsman,
  Fell the ship-crews
  Doomed to the death.

[1] I have more or less availed myself of my son's prose translation of
this poem in the *Contemporary Review* (November 1876).
[2] Shields of linden-wood.

All the field with blood of the fighters
     Flowed, from when first the great
     Sun-star of morning-tide,
     Lamp of the Lord God
     Lord everlasting,
Glode over earth till the glorious creature
     Sank to his setting.

IV

     There lay many a man
     Marred by the javelin,
     Men of the Northland
     Shot over shield.
     There was the Scotsman
     Weary of war.

V

     We the West-Saxons,   20
     Long as the daylight
     Lasted, in companies
Troubled the track of the host that we hated.
Grimly with swords that were sharp from the grind-
    stone,
Fiercely we hacked at the flyers before us.

VI

     Mighty the Mercian,
     Hard was his hand-play,
     Sparing not any of
     Those that with Anlaf,
     Warriors over the
     Weltering waters

Borne in the bark's-bosom,
Drew to this island —
Doomed to the death.

VII

30   Five young kings put asleep by the sword-stroke,
Seven strong Earls of the army of Anlaf
Fell on the war-field, numberless numbers,
Shipmen and Scotsmen.

VIII

Then the Norse leader,
Dire was his need of it,
Few were his following,
Fled to his war-ship;
Fleeted his vessel to sea with the king in it,
Saving his life on the fallow flood.

IX

Also the crafty one,
Constantinus,
Crept to his North again,
Hoar-headed hero!

X

40   Slender warrant had
He to be proud of
The welcome of war-knives —
He that was reft of his
Folk and his friends that had
Fallen in conflict,
Leaving his son too

Lost in the carnage,
Mangled to morsels,
A youngster in war !

XI

Slender reason had
He to be glad of
The clash of the war-glaive —
Traitor and trickster
And spurner of treaties —
He nor had Anlaf
With armies so broken
A reason for bragging
That they had the better
In perils of battle
On places of slaughter —
The struggle of standards,
The rush of the javelins,
The crash of the charges,[1]   50
The wielding of weapons —
The play that they played with
The children of Edward.

XII

Then with their nailed prows
Parted the Norsemen, a
Blood-reddened relic of
Javelins over
The jarring breaker, the deep-sea billow,
Shaping their way toward Dyflen[2] again,
Shamed in their souls.

[1] Lit. 'the gathering of men.'   [2] Dublin.

XIII

Also the brethren,
King and Atheling,
Each in his glory,
Went to his own in his own West-Saxonland,
Glad of the war.

XIV

60   Many a carcase they left to be carrion,
Many a livid one, many a sallow-skin —
Left for the white-tailed eagle to tear it, and
Left for the horny-nibbed raven to rend it, and
Gave to the garbaging war-hawk to gorge it, and
That gray beast, the wolf of the weald.

XV

Never had huger
Slaughter of heroes
Slain by the sword-edge —
Such as old writers
Have writ of in histories —
Hapt in this isle, since
Up from the East hither
70   Saxon and Angle from
Over the broad billow
Broke into Britain with
Haughty war-workers who
Harried the Welshman, when
Earls that were lured by the
Hunger of glory gat
Hold of the land.

ALFRED TENNYSON.

THE BATTLE OF MALDON

In the *Saxon Chronicle*, under the year 991, we are told: 'This year came Unlaf [Olaf Tryggvason] with ninety-three ships to Staines, and laid waste all around ; and thence he went to Sandwich, and thence to Ipswich, and harried it all, and so to Maldon, and there Byrhtnoth the earl and his force came against him and fought with him; and there they slew the earl and kept the battlefield. And in that year they decided to pay tribute for the first time to the Danes, on account of the great terror which they wrought on the sea-coast; this tribute was at first ten thousand pounds.'

The scene of the poem is Maldon in Essex, or rather the village of Heybridge near by.   Here two rivers come together — the Blackwater, formerly called the Panta, and the Chelmer.   According to Freeman, Byrhtnoth came to the rescue from the north.   Olaf (b. 969), the favorite hero of Norse history, is the same that is celebrated in Longfellow's *Saga of King Olaf.* Æthelred is King Æthelred the Unready (968–1016).   Of the warriors of the poem, except Byrhtnoth, nothing is certainly known.

Useful hints concerning the battle may be found in Lumsden's article in *Macmillan's Magazine* 55 371, and in Freeman, *Norman Conquest*, Vol. 1.   Other discussions of value are by Abegg, *Zur Entwicklung der Historischen Dichtung bei den Angelsachsen*, Strassburg, 1894, and by Liebermann, in *Herrig's Archiv* 101 15–29.   According to the latter, this battle took place on August 11, 991.   Byrhtnoth was Earl (*ealdorman*) of the East Saxons, and his force was the East-Saxon militia.

The best edition, containing also *The Battle of Brunanburh*, is by Sedgefield (Boston, 1904), who says (p. vii): 'Very striking is the absence of ornament from the *Battle of Maldon*; all is plain, blunt, stern.'

31

· · · · · ·

He bade each youth turn loose his horse and drive it
    far away,
And onward go with steadfast heart to mingle in the fray.
  When Offa's kinsman saw the Earl no cowardice would
    brook,
Off from his wrist to woodland wide his falcon dear he
    shook;
He joined the ranks, and straightway then might all men
    clearly know
10 Never the knight would shrink from fight when armed
    against the foe.
  Beside his liege lord Eadric, too, in battle sought
    to be;
Forth to the war he bore his spear — a dauntless heart
    had he —
The while he with his hands could grasp the buckler and
    broad sword;
Right well he kept the vow he pledged to fight before
    his lord.
  There Byrhtnoth [1] then arrayed his men and taught
    them how to stand,
20 To keep their ranks, and fearless grasp the buckler in
    the hand.
And when they were in order set, he lighted from his
    steed
Among his own loved household-men whom he knew
    good at need.
  The herald of the Vikings stood beside the river shore,

---

[1] Changed throughout from the 'Brihtnoth' of Lumsden. — EDS.

And the sea-rover's haughty words before the Earl he
    bore:
'From seamen bold I come: they bid that thou shalt 30
    straightway send
Treasure for ransom; better 'twill be for you in the end
To buy with gifts our onslaught off than with us war to
    hold.
No need to fight if ye agree — we'll make a peace for
    gold:
If so thou orderest it, who here among the rest art chief,
That thou wilt set thy people free, then bid for their
    relief,
That they shall to the seamen give as seamen shall decree
Treasure for peace; then take ye peace, and we will put
    to sea
With booty-laden ships, and peace henceforth between 40
    us be!'
   Then Byrhtnoth lifted up his voice — his shield he
    brandished high,
And shook his slender ashen shaft — and thus he made
    reply.
Wrathful and resolute he spake: 'O thou sea-robber,
    hear
What saith this folk! To you they give no tribute but
    the spear,
The venomed point, the old keen edge, and all the
    battle-gear
That works no good for you in fight! Go, seamen's
    herald, say
This message of yet deeper hate: that here, an Earl, 50
    I stay

Undaunted with my men to guard the kingdom, folk,
and land

Of Æthelred my lord. In war the heathen shall not stand!

That ye should with our spoil go hence unfought, since
thus ye came

So far into this land of ours, too great meseems the
shame!

Nor think ye to win gold with ease — rather shall grim
war-play

60 And sword and spear our compact make ere we will
tribute pay!'

   With that he bade his men go forth; their bucklers
then they bore

Till at the landing-place they stood beside the river-shore.

Neither could reach the other there — between them
flowed the tide;

For after ebb the flood rolled up, it filled the channel wide.

And till their spears together clashed too long the time
did seem

To Vikings and East-Saxon ranks arrayed by Panta's
stream,

70 For neither could the other hurt save by the arrows'
flight

Till ebb of tide.   Then ready there and burning for the
fight

The Vikings stood, the seamen host.   But Wulfstan —
warrior old,

The son of Ceola — with his kin by Byrhtnoth sent to
hold

The bridge against them, with the lance the foremost
Viking slew

Who stepped, foolhardy, on the bridge. With Wulfstan
    heroes two,

Ælfhere·and Maccus, firmly stood, no passage would 80
    they yield,

But bravely fought against the foe while they could
    weapons wield.

  Now when the hated strangers saw the bridge-wards
      there so stout,

They changed their ground, and to the ford they led
    their forces out.

Then for the heathen host the Earl made way, and overbold 90

Men heard the son of Byrhthelm shout across the waters
    cold :

'Lo! here is room for you! Come on, come warriors to
    the fray!

God only knows which of us twain shall hold the field
    to-day.'

Then onward came the wolves of war, they recked not
    of the flood ;

Westward o'er Panta's gleaming waves they bore their
    shields and stood

Upon the bank. There 'gainst their foes were Byrht- 100
    noth's men arrayed,

And at his word they held their ground and buckler-
    wail they made.

  Now drew the time of glorious deeds, the tide of battle
      nigh ;

And now the fatal hour was come when death-doomed
    men must die!

Now loud uprose the battle-cry, and, greedy for their
    prey,

The ravens wheeled, the eagles screamed. On earth
   was noise of fray!
  From hand was hurled the sharp-filed spear, the
    whetted arrow flew,
110 The bow was busy, shield met spear, and fierce the
   combat grew,
On either side brave soldiers fell. There Byrhtnoth's
   kinsman died,
Wulfmær, his sister's son, all hewn with sword-wounds
   deep and wide.
But to the Vikings recompense was fully paid; I know
That Eadward smote one with his sword, nor did the
   stroke forego
120 Till at his feet the doomed foe lay.   For this his lord
   gave thanks
To his bower-thane in season due.   Thus stoutly in the
   ranks
The warriors fought with weapons sharp, and each one
   strove to be
The first whose spear might reach the life of death-
   doomed enemy.
On earth was slaughter!   Firm they stood; and Byrhtnoth's words of flame
Stirred every heart to bide the brunt and win a glorious
   name.
130   Forth went the hero old in war, he raised his shelter-
    ing shield
And shook his spear, and onward went into the battle-
   field.
Thus of one mind went earl to churl — alike their fell
   intent.

A southern lance the warrior's lord now pierced, by
  Viking sent;
But with his shield he thrust at it, the shaft to splinters
  broke,
And bent the head till out it sprang; then fierce his
  wrath awoke,
And at the foe who dealt the wound he hurled his
  deadly spear.
Skilled was the leader of the host — he sent the javelin 140
  sheer
Through the youth's neck; his guiding hand that Viking
  sought to slay;
And then another swift he shot, through corslet it made
  way,
And in the heart through rings of mail the venomed
  lance-head stood.
The blither was the Earl for that — he laughed, the
  bold of mood,
And for the day's work rendered thanks that God to
  him had given.
  But from a warrior's clenchèd hand a dart was fiercely 150
  driven,
Too sure it went, and pierced the noble thane of Æthelred.
Besides him stood a beardless youth — a boy in battle
  dread —
Young Wulfmær, son of Wulfstan; he swift from the
  hero drew
The bloody dart and hurled it back; the hardened spear-
  head flew,
And on the earth the Viking lay who thus had reached
  his lord.

Then rushed a warrior armed to seize the goodly graven
    sword,
160 Bracelets, and corslet of the Earl, but Byrhtnoth drew
    his blade,
Brown-edged and broad, and fierce the strokes he on his
    corslet laid.
Too soon another smote his arm and hindered him.
    Then rolled
On earth the yellow-hilted sword, nor longer could he hold
Keen blade, nor weapon wield ; but still the gray-haired
    leader bade
170 His men keep heart and onward press, good comrades
    undismayed.
    No longer could he stand upright, his eyes to heaven
      he bent :
'Ruler of nations!   I give thanks for all that Thou hast
    lent
Of joys in this world.   Now have I, O gracious Lord!
    most need
That Thou show favor to my soul, that it to Thee may
    speed,
And to Thy kingdom, Lord of angels! pass in peace.
    I pray
180 That hell-foes do me no despite.'
                         They hewed him as he lay —
The heathen dogs! — and two with him, Ælfnoth and
    Wulfmær ; there
Beside their lord they gave their lives.   Then those who
    did not dare
To bide the battle turned away, and foremost in the
    flight

Were Odda's sons: Godric forsook his leader and the
    fight;
On his lord's horse he basely leaped — he who from that 190
    kind man
Had many a horse received — and with him both his
    brothers ran.
Godrinc and Godwy turned and fled, they cared not for
    the strife,
But sought the fastness of the wood and saved their
    coward life!
And many more ran with them than beseemed if they
    had thought
Of all the good in happier times the Earl for them had
    wrought,
So in the mead-hall at the moot had Offa said one day,
That many there spoke boldly who at need would fall 200
    away.
Thus fell the leader of the host, the Earl of Æthelred,
And all his hearth-companions saw that there their lord
    lay dead.
  But hotly thither came proud thanes and dauntless
    men drew nigh;
One thing alone they all desired — to take revenge or die!
Young Ælfwine, Ælfric's son was he, thus boldly spake 210
    to all
And cheered them on: 'O think how oft we've sat —
    brave men in hall! —
And on the benches o'er the mead made boast of deeds
    in fight!
Now let the truly brave be seen! I will in all men's
    sight

Uphold my ancestry ; I come of noble Mercian race,
Ealhelm my grandsire was — a ruler wise and high in
　　place ;
220 And never shall my people's thanes reproach me that
　　I fled
To seek my native land, and left my leader lying dead —
To me the worst of ills, for he my kinsman was and lord !'
Then forward burning for revenge he rushed, and with
　　his sword
He smote a seaman 'mong the foe (on earth the heathen
　　lay
Hewn with the weapon) and he cheered his comrades to
　　the fray.
230 'Ælfwine, well said !' cried Offa then, and shook his
　　ashen spear,
'Full surely it behoves us all, when slain our lord lies here,
To cheer each other on to fight while we can weapons
　　wield,
Good sword, hard brand, or lance ! Nigh lost to us hath
　　been the field
Through Godric, Odda's dastard son ; when on the noble
　　steed
240 He rode away, too many deemed it was our lord indeed,
And thus the folk were all dismayed — broken the
　　buckler-wall ;
On his foul deed that wrought such flight my curses
　　ever fall !'
　　Leofsunu to the warriors spake and raised his linden
　　　shield :
'A vow I've made that one foot's length here will I
　　never yield,

But to revenge my dear loved lord right onward will I
    fare!
Round Stourmere never shall they say — the sturdy
    fighters there —
The scornful words that, now my lord is fallen, I turned 25c
    from fray
And went home lordless! No! me rather spear and
    sword shall slay!'
Wrathful he rushed, he scorned to flee, but fought with
    steadfast heart.
    Dunhere (an aged churl was he) then spoke and shook
        his dart ;
Each warrior to revenge the earl he bade, and loud o'er
    all,
'Let him,' he cried, 'who on the foe would wreak his
    leader's fall
Brook no delay, nor care for life!' And onward went 260
    they then —
Regardless of their lives they went. Fiercely the house-
    hold men,
The grim spear-bearers fought ; to God they prayed that
    they might take
Full vengeance on their enemies for their loved leader's
    sake.
    The hostage Æscferth, Ecglaf's son, now helped them
        readily,
(Of stout Northumbrian race he came); never at all
    paused he
In war-play, but continually he let his arrows go ;
Sometimes with them he struck a shield, and sometimes 270
    pierced a foe ;

With every shot he dealt a wound while he could weapons
     wield.
  Eager and fierce tall Eadward stood, the foremost in
     the field,
Never a foot length would he flee, thus haughtily he spoke,
Nor turn his back on his dead lord!   The buckler-wall
     he broke,
And fought the foe till, ere he died, full vengeance he
     had wrought,
For his wealth-giver, on the Danes.   And fiercely like-
     wise fought
280 His noble comrade Sigbyrht's brother Ætheric, brave
     and true,
And many more; the keelèd shields they clove, they
     sternly slew.
All broken was the buckler's edge — dreadful the cors-
     lets' song!
  Now Offa struck and felled to earth a seaman 'mid
     the throng,
But there Gadd's kinsman bit the dust — too soon was
     Offa slain!
290 Yet he fulfilled the vow he pledged his lord that both
     again
Should ride safe homeward to the burgh, or wounded in
     the fray
Die on the battle-field.   Thane-like, beside his lord, he
     lay!
  Loud clashed the shields!   Oft went the spear through
     doomed man's house of life!
The Vikings, burning for the war, came on.   Then to
     the strife

Wigstan the son of Thurstan rushed, and in the crowd
   slew three
Ere he lay dead.   'Twas fiercest moot!   The warriors 300
   steadfastly
In battle stood and wounded fell.   On earth was slaughter
   dire !
Oswald and Ealdwold all the while still kept the ranks
   entire,
And both the brothers with fit words besought their
   kinsmen dear
Unflinchingly to bide the brunt and wield the sword and
   spear.
   Then Byrhtwold the old comrade spoke ; he shook his 310
      ashen dart
And grasped his shield and proudly cried : 'The bolder
   be each heart,
Each spirit sterner, valor more, now that our strength
   is less !
Here our good leader lies on earth ; may he who now
   from stress
Of war-play turns, for ever rue !   Full old of years am I —
Hence will I never, but beside my lord I hope to lie,
The man beloved ! '
                     So Godric, too, the son of Æthelgar, 320
Cheered on the warriors to the fight.   Oft flew his spear
   afar —
His deadly spear — and Vikings smote : then rushing on
   the foe
Foremost of all he cut and hewed till battle laid him low.
Not that same Godric he who turned from fight.   .   .

                         H. W. LUMSDEN.

II

SECULAR LYRICS

THE SEAFARER

Date and author unknown. The German scholar Rieger suggested (1869) that the poem was a dialogue between an old mariner and a young man who longed to go to sea, the parts being thus distributed (O=old, Y=young): O. 1–33 (*grain*); Y. 33–38; O. 39–47; Y. 48–52 (*tides*); O. 53–57 (*exile*); Y. 58–71 (*depart*); O. 71–124. Kluge recognizes (1883, 1885) only two dramatic speeches: O. 1–33; Y. 33–64 (or 66), regarding what follows as by another author, who unskilfully combines homiletical and gnomic sentences with a bit of elegy (80ᵇ–93, *The days — earth*), certain lines being wholly or partially unintelligible.

Sieper (*Die Altenglische Elegie*, Strassburg, 1915, pp. 182–195) reviews the principal studies of the poem which regard it as consisting of two disparate parts, but comes to no very satisfactory result. Among those scholars who have conceived of it as a unit are Ten Brink (*Early English Literature*, p. 63) and Ebert. Certain of the Polar explorers have displayed a spirit not unlike that manifested in this poem (cf. Tennyson, *Sir John Franklin*).

PART I

I can sing of myself a true song, of my voyages telling,
How oft through laborious days, through the wearisome
    hours
I have suffered; have borne tribulations; explored in
    my ship,

Mid the terrible rolling of waves, habitations of sorrow.
Benumbed by the cold, oft the comfortless night-watch
    hath held me
At the prow of my craft as it tossed about under the
    cliffs.
My feet were imprisoned with frost, were fettered with
    ice-chains,
Yet hotly were wailing the querulous sighs round my 10
    heart ;
And hunger within me, sea-wearied, made havoc of
    courage.
    This he, whose lot happily chances on land, doth not
      know ;
Nor how I on the ice-cold sea passed the winter in exile,
In wretchedness, robbed of my kinsmen, with icicles
    hung.
The hail flew in showers about me; and there I heard
    only
The roar of the sea, ice-cold waves, and the song of the
    swan ;
For pastime the gannets' cry served me; the kittiwakes' 20
    chatter
For laughter of men; and for mead-drink the call of the
    sea-mews.
When storms on the rocky cliffs beat, then the terns,
    icy-feathered,
Made answer; full oft the sea-eagle forebodingly
    screamed,
The eagle with pinions wave-wet. There none of my
    kinsmen
Might gladden my desolate soul ; of this little he knows

Who possesses the pleasures of life, who has felt in the
      city
Some hardship, some trifling adversity, proud and wine-
      flushed.
30   How weary I oft had to tarry upon the sea-way!
The shadows of night became darker, it snowed from
      the north;
The world was enchained by the frost; hail fell upon
      earth;
'Twas the coldest of grain.   Yet the thoughts of my
      heart now are throbbing
To test the high streams, the salt waves in tumultuous
      play.
Desire in my heart ever urges my spirit to wander
To seek out the home of the stranger in lands afar off.
   There is no one that dwells upon earth, so exalted in
      mind,
40 So large in his bounty, nor yet of such vigorous youth,
Nor so daring in deeds, nor to whom his liege lord is so
      kind,
But that he has always a longing, a sea-faring passion
For what the Lord God shall bestow, be it honor or
      death.
No heart for the harp has he, nor for acceptance of
      treasure,
No pleasure has he in a wife, no delight in the world,
Nor in aught save the roll of the billows; but always a
      longing,
A yearning uneasiness, hastens him on to the sea.
   The woodlands are captured by blossoms, the hamlets
      grow fair,

Broad meadows are beautiful, earth again bursts into
    life,
And all stir the heart of the wanderer eager to journey, 50
So he meditates going afar on the pathway of tides.
The cuckoo, moreover, gives warning with sorrowful
    note,
Summer's harbinger sings, and forebodes to the heart
    bitter sorrow.
The nobleman comprehends not, the luxurious man,
What some must endure, who travel the farthest in exile.
  Now my spirit uneasily turns in the heart's narrow
    chamber,
Now wanders forth over the tide, o'er the home of the 60
    whale,
To the ends of the earth — and comes back to me.
    Eager and greedy,
The lone wanderer screams, and resistlessly drives my
    soul onward,
Over the whale-path, over the tracts of the sea.

PART II

The delights of the Lord are far dearer to me than this
    dead,
Fleeting life upon earth, for I can not believe that earth's
    riches
For ever endure.   Each one of three things, ere its time
    comes,
Is always uncertain : violence, age, and disease   70
Wrench the soul away, doomed to depart. This is praise
    from the living,

From those who speak afterwards, this the best fame
after death —

That ere he departed he labored, and wrought daring
deeds

'Gainst the malice of fiends, and the devil; so men shall
extol him,

His praise among angels shall live, ever, world without
end,

80 His the blessing of life everlasting, and joy mid the hosts.

The days have departed, all pomps of earth's kingdom
have vanished;

There now are no kings, no emperors now, no gold-
givers

As of yore, when they wrought in their midst the most
glorious deeds,

And lived in the lordliest power. This glory has fallen,

Delights have all vanished away; the weak ones remain,

And these govern the world, obtaining their pleasure
with effort.

Power has declined, earth's glory grows aged and sear,

90 Like every man now in the world; old age overtakes him,

His countenance loses its color, gray-haired he laments;

He has seen his old friends, sons of princes, consigned
to the earth.

This garment of flesh has no power, when the spirit
escapes,

To drink in the sweet nor to taste of the bitter; it then

Has no power to stretch forth the hands or to think with
the mind.

Though the grave should be covered with gold by the
nearest of kin,

Be buried along with the dead in masses of treasure,
Still that will not go with them.   Gold can no substitute
    be
For the fear of the Lord, to the soul which is laden with 100
    sin,
Which aforetime, so long as it lived, kept that treasure
    concealed.
    Great is the fear of the Lord;   the earth trembles
       before it ;
He established the unmovable earth, the world and the
    heavens.
Foolish is he who stands not in awe of the Lord —
Unexpectedly death comes upon him ; but happy is he
Who lives humble in mind, to him cometh honor from
    heaven ;
God doth establish the soul that believes in His might.
    One should check a strong will, and should govern it
       firmly,
Be true unto men, and be clean in his manner of life. . . . 110
Fate, God the Creator, is stronger than any man's will.
    Come, let us reflect where our home is, consider the
       way
By which we go thither; then let us each strive to press
    forward
To joy everlasting, where life has its source in God's love, 120
Where is heavenly hope.   Then to Him who is holy be
    thanks,
Because He hath honored us ; thanks to the Ruler of
    Heaven,
The Lord everlasting, throughout all the ages! Amen.

LaMotte Iddings.

THE WANDERER

The poem is not a romantic picture of one who is 'ever wandering with a hungry heart' (as *The Seafarer*, with which it should be compared, is not about a sailor), but simply the lament of a professional poet who has lost his patron by death, and whose lot, in his vain attempt to find another, is little better than that of an exile. The theme of the passing of earthly joy blends easily with the Christian doctrine of the transitoriness of this life. Compare especially pp. 19, 44, 56.

A detailed study of the poem is provided by R. Imelmann in his *Forschungen zur Altenglischen Poesie*, Berlin, 1920.

'Still the lone one and desolate waits for his Maker's
    ruth —
God's good mercy, albeit so long it tarry, in sooth.
Careworn and sad of heart, on the watery ways must he
Plow with the hand-grasped oar — how long? — the
    rime-cold sea,
Tread thy paths of exile, O Fate, who art cruelty.'
    Thus did a wanderer speak, being heart-full of woe,
    and all
Thoughts of the cruel slayings, and pleasant comrades'
    fall:
'Morn by morn I, alone, am fain to utter my woe;
Now is there none of the living to whom I dare to show
10 Plainly the thought of my heart; in very sooth I know
Excellent is it in man that his breast he straightly bind,

Shut fast his thinkings in silence, whatever he have in
 his mind.
The man that is weary in heart, he never can fate with-
 stand ;
The man that grieves in his spirit, he finds not the
 helper's hand.
Therefore the glory-grasper full heavy of soul may be.
So, far from my fatherland, and mine own good kinsmen 20
 free,
I must bind my heart in fetters, for long, ah ! long ago,
The earth's cold darkness covered my giver of gold
 brought low ;
And I, sore stricken and humbled, and winter-saddened,
 went
Far over the frost-bound waves to seek for the dear
 content
Of the hall of the giver of rings ; but far nor near could
 I find
Who felt the love of the mead-hall, or who with comforts
 kind
Would comfort me, the friendless. 'T is he alone will
 know,
Who knows, being desolate too, how evil a fere is woe ; 30
For him the path of the exile, and not the twisted gold ;
For him the frost in his bosom, and not earth-riches old.
 'O, well he remembers the hall-men, the treasure
  bestowed in the hall ;
The feast that his gold-giver made him, the joy at its
 highth, at its fall ;
He knows who must be forlorn for his dear lord's
 counsels gone,

40 Where sleep and sorrow together are binding the lonely
     one ;
When himthinks he clasps and kisses his leader of men,
     and lays
His hands and head on his knee, as when, in the good
     yore-days.
He sat on the throne of his might, in the strength that
     wins and saves.
But the friendless man awakes, and he sees the yellow
     waves,
And the sea-birds dip to the sea, and broaden their wings
     to the gale,
And he sees the dreary rime, and the snow commingled
     with hail.

50 O, then are the wounds of his heart the sorer much
     for this,
The grief for the loved and lost made new by the dream
     of old bliss.
His kinsmen's memory comes to him as he lies asleep,
And he greets it with joy, with joy, and the heart in his
     breast doth leap ;
But out of his ken the shapes of his warrior-comrades
     swim
To the land whence seafarers bring no dear old saws for
     him ;
Then fresh grows sorrow and new to him whose bitter
     part
Is to send o'er the frost-bound waves full often his weary
     heart.
For this do I look around this world, and cannot see
Wherefore or why my heart should not grow dark in me.

When I think of the lives of the leaders, the clansmen 60
    mighty in mood ;
When I think how sudden and swift they yielded the
    place where they stood.
So droops this mid-earth and falls, and never a man is
    found
Wise ere a many winters have girt his life around.
Full patient the sage must be, and he that would counsel
    teach —
Not over-hot in his heart, nor over-swift in his speech ;
Nor faint of soul nor secure, nor fain for the fight nor
    afraid ;
Nor ready to boast before he know himself well arrayed.
The proud-souled man must bide when he utters his 70
    vaunt, until
He know of the thoughts of the heart, and whitherward
    turn they will.
The prudent must understand how terror and awe
    shall be,
When the glory and weal of the world lie waste, as now
    men see
On our mid-earth, many a where, the wind-swept walls
    arise,
And the ruined dwellings and void, and the rime that on
    them lies.[1]
The wine-halls crumble, bereft of joy the warriors lie,
The flower of the doughty fallen, the proud ones fair to
    the eye.
War took off some in death, and one did a strong bird 80
    bear

[1] Cf. *The Ruined City*, p. 56.

Over the deep; and one — his bones did the gray wolf
    share ;

And one was hid in a cave by a comrade sorrowful-
    faced.

O, thus the Shaper of men hath laid the earth all
    waste,

Till the works of the city-dwellers, the works of the
    giants of earth,

Stood empty and lorn of the burst of the mighty revelers'
    mirth.

    'Who wisely hath mused on this wallstead, and
        ponders this dark life well,

90 In his heart he hath often bethought him of slayings
    many and fell,

And these be the words he taketh, the thoughts of his
    heart to tell :

"Where is the horse and the rider?[1]   Where is the giver
    of gold ?

Where be the seats at the banquet ?   Where be the hall-
    joys of old ?

Alas for the burnished cup, for the byrnied chief to-day!

Alas for the strength of the prince ! for the time hath
    passed away —

Is hid 'neath the shadow of night, as it never had been
    at all.

Behind the dear and doughty there standeth now a wall,

A wall that is wondrous high, and with wondrous snake-
    work wrought.

The strength of the spears hath fordone the earls and
    hath made them naught,

---

[1] Cf. *Beowulf* 2455 ff.

The weapons greedy of slaughter, and she, the mighty 100
    Wyrd ;
And the tempests beat on the rocks, and the storm-wind
    that maketh afeard —
The terrible storm that fetters the earth, the winter-
    bale,
When the shadow of night falls wan, and wild is the
    rush of the hail,
The cruel rush from the north, which maketh men to
    quail.
Hardship-full is the earth, o'erturned when the stark
    Wyrds say :
Here is the passing of riches, here friends are passing
    away ;
And men and kinsfolk pass, and nothing and none may
    stay ;
And all this earth-stead here shall be empty and void 110
    one day." . .'

EMILY H. HICKEY.

THE RUINED CITY

A fragmentary poem of forty-eight lines, whose date and author are unknown. References to hot springs (ll. 39, 41) naturally suggest Bath as the city described. Bath may have been plundered by the Saxons; in the *Chronicle*, under date 577, we read, ' This year Cuthwine and Ceawline fought against the Britons — and took three cities from them, Gloucester, and Cirencester, and Bath.'

R. G. Collingwood (*Roman Britain*, London, 1923, p. 58) writes: ' The towns of Roman Britain seem as a rule to have perished more or less violently about the beginning of the fifth century, and when, some time later, the Anglo-Saxon settlements gradually began, the towns were mostly, perhaps all, blackened and silent ruins. Nor were the new settlers quick to rebuild them; for they were not by habit or inclination town-dwellers.' It will be noticed that the poet's interest is elicited by the fact that the walls are of stone, and relics of an age of greater men and mightier builders. Heorot, the wooden palace of King Hrothgar, was, like this towered city, ' high and pinnacled,' but destined also to be destroyed (*Beowulf* 81 ff. Cf. p. 16, above).

Wondrously wrought and fair its wall of stone,
Shattered by Fate ! The castles rend asunder,
The work of giants moldereth away,
Its roofs are breaking and falling ; its towers crumble
In ruin. Plundered those walls with grated doors —
Their mortar white with frost. Its battered ramparts
Are shorn away and ruined, all undermined
By eating age. The mighty men that built it,
Departed hence, undone by death, are held
Fast in the earth's embrace. Tight is the clutch

Of the grave, while overhead for living men
A hundred generations pass away.

Long this red wall, now mossy gray, withstood,   10
While kingdom followed kingdom in the land,
Unshaken 'neath the storms of heaven — yet now
Its towering gate hath fallen. . . .

Radiant the mead-halls in that city bright,
Yea, many were its baths.   High rose its wealth
Of hornèd pinnacles, while loud within
Was heard the joyous revelry of men —
Till mighty Fate came with her sudden change!   25

Wide-wasting was the battle where they fell.
Plague-laden days upon the city came;
Death snatched away that mighty host of men.[1] . .

There in the olden time full many a thane,
Shining with gold, all gloriously adorned,
Haughty in heart, rejoiced when hot with wine;
Upon him gleamed his armor, and he gazed
On gold and silver and all precious gems;
On riches and on wealth and treasured jewels,
A radiant city in a kingdom wide.

There stood the courts of stone.   Hotly within,
The stream flowed with its mighty surge.   The wall   40
Surrounded all with its bright bosom; there
The baths stood, hot within its heart. . . .

CHAUNCEY B. TINKER.

[1] Several exceedingly obscure lines are omitted at this point.

DEOR'S LAMENT

The experience of Deor, a professional bard, in being displaced by a poet of the newer school, results in a state of mind not unlike that of the *Wanderer* (p. 50). This poem, which has the unusual features of strophe and refrain, has also been studied by Imelmann (cf. p. 50). It is remarkable for its references to mythological and historical persons (Wayland and Theodoric), for whom reference may be made to Vigfusson and Powell's *Corpus Poeticum Boreale* **1** 168 ff. For the other myths, consult G. Binz's *Zeugnisse zur Germanischen Sage in England*, in Paul and Braune's *Beiträge* **20** 141 ff.

(A free paraphrase.)

Weland, the constant-hearted, knew well what sorrow
 meant,
When woman's vengeance laid him low and woke his
 long lament.
Grief was his life-long comrade; he felt her cold
 caress
When Nithhad lamed his limbs and on him laid that
 long distress.
Yet he strove on, and overcame; nor shall *my* strength
 be less.

And on the breast of Beadohild her brothers' murder
 lay
Less heavy than her own soul's grief, when on that
 hateful day

58

Her heart first knew what burden her outraged body
    bore,
Awaking from that hideous dream, her woe for ever-
    more.
Yet she strove on, and overcame ; shall I my griefs
    deplore ?

All know Hild's shameful fortune and that god's
    unfathomed sorrow
Who through love's wakeful years of night watched
    weeping for the morrow ;
All know how King Theodoric, by that accursèd spell,
Kept, motionless, for thirty years, the Mærings'
    citadel.
Yet these strove on, and overcame ; I can endure as
    well.

And all have heard of Eormanric, king of the wolfish
    heart,
Who scourged the Gothic kingdoms, and made his
    subjects smart ;
And many a man of sorrows, with sudden woe oppressed,
Cried bitterly for vengeance as he beat his stricken
    breast.
Yet these strove on, and overcame ; shall I not stand
    the test ?

(Outcast, and sorrowing in his soul,
The aged harper chants his dole,
And, o'er the strings his gray head bending,
Sees in his heart but woe unending.

Let him remember, and take cheer;
The good Lord God of heaven draws near,
Who for our sowing gives just reaping,
And makes an end of this world's weeping.)

I, Deor of the Heodenings, was dear to my good lord,
And did long minstrel service, nor missed my due
reward;
40   Till now this mightier minstrel thrusts my lord and
me apart,
And wins my lands and living with the wiles of his
high art.
He has his day; he overcame; but peace! break not,
my heart!

CHARLTON M. LEWIS.

A LOVE–LETTER

The poem falls into two parts, lines 1–17 and lines 18–70. The first of these is a description by the letter itself — *i. e.* the slip of bark or wood on which the message is carved — of its former life and its transformation into its present guise; the second part contains the message of the lover. Throughout it is the letter, not the lover, that speaks. This relation has not been generally recognized. The parts were formerly designated respectively as *Riddle 61 (60)* and *The Husband's Message*. The present arrangement was suggested by Professor F. A. Blackburn in the *Journal of Germanic Philology* **3** 1 ff., where this translation is found. See the comments by Tupper (p. 199), and Wyatt (pp. 108–110), in their editions of the Old English riddles.

The runes at lines 66, 67 are supposed to be a cipher or password sent to the lady.

My home was on the beach near the sea-shore ;
Beside the ocean's brim I dwelt, fast fixed
In my first abode.   Few of mankind there were
That there beheld my home in the solitude,
But every morn the brown wave encircled me
With its watery embrace.   Little weened I then
That I should ever, earlier or later,
Though mouthless, speak among the mead-drinkers
And utter words.   A great marvel it is,
Strange in the mind that knoweth it not,   10
How the point of the knife and the right hand,
The thought of a man, and his blade therewith,

Shaped me with skill, that boldly I might
So deliver a message to thee
In the presence of us two alone,
That to other men our talk
May not make it more widely known.
   Now to thee will I tell apart
That I sprang from the stock of the tree-race.
20   In other lands the skill of man is wont
To set on me cunning characters.
Then in a vessel I traverse the salt waves;
Oft in the prison of a ship have I visited lands,
Where my lord has sent me,
And lofty castles.   Now am I come hither
In the keeled vessel, and now shalt thou know
How thou mayest think in thy heart
Of the love of my lord.   I dare maintain
That there thou wilt find true loyalty.
30   Lo! he that carved this stave bade me
Pray thee, O jewel-decked, to remember
In thy heart the word-pledges,
Which in days of yore ye two oft spake,
While in the mead-castles ye were permitted
To have a home, to dwell in the same land,
To practice friendship.   Force drove him
Out of the land.   Now hath he bidden me
Earnestly to urge thee to sail the sea
When thou hast heard on the brow of the hill
40   The mournful cuckoo call in the wood.
Then let no living man keep thee
From the journey or hinder thy going.
Betake thee to the sea, the home of the mew;

Seat thee in the boat, that southward from here
Beyond the road of the sea thou mayest find the man
Where waits thy prince in hope of thee.
No joy of the world can be greater for him
In his thoughts, as he hath told me,
Than that the all-ruling God should grant you
That ye together should hereafter 50
Give out treasure to men and comrades,
Golden rings.   Enough he hath
Of beaten gold, of wealth and treasure,
Since among strangers he hath a home,
A fair abode ; there obey him many
Noble warriors, though here my banished lord,
Driven by necessity, pushed out his boat
And on the path of the waves was forced to run,
To journey on the water-way, eager for escape,
To stir the waves.   Now hath the man 60
Overcome his trouble ; he hath no lack of pleasures,
Of steeds or of jewels, or of mead-joys,
Or of any treasure on earth,
O prince's daughter, if he have thee
In spite of the old threat against you both.
    I put together S   R
EA   W   and   M(D?), to assure thee with an oath
That while he lives he will fulfill
The pledge and the love-troth
That in days of old ye often spake. 70

Francis A. Blackburn.

THE BANISHED WIFE'S COMPLAINT

Date and author unknown.   Trautmann (*Anglia* **16** 207 ff.) sug-
gests that *The Wife's Complaint* and *The Husband's Message* (see
above, p. 61 : *A Love-Letter*) are only fragments of one long narra-
tive.   The poem is, however, quite comprehensible in its present
form.   As a purely dramatic utterance, it may serve to remind us
of the rashness of regarding such monologues (cf. pp. 50, 58) as
referring to personal experiences of the poets who wrote them.

In solitude I sing this lonely song
About my fate ; and truly can I say
That of the ills encountered since my youth,
Ills new and old, most grievous far is this —
Sorrows of endless exile I endure !
   Erstwhile my lord departed from the people
Over the billows' strife.   Dawn after dawn
I tossed in anguish, asking in myself :
' Where lies the land to which my lord has gone ? '
Deeper grew my distress, until at length,
A friendless fugitive, I took my way,
Troubled beyond relief, to seek for him.
The kindred of that man through cunning thought
Baseless dissension built betwixt us two,
That hatefully divided we should dwell
Within the world ; and woe untold was mine.
   By my lord's mandate here I made my home.
Few loving ones I had in this landstead,

Few gracious friends.   Wherefore is my great grief,
That him, most fitting of all men for me,
False-hearted I have found and treacherous ;   20
With loving smile devising deadly sin.
Often we promised faithfully that love
Should last with life, that separation naught
But death alone should bring — how different now !
Our friendship is as it had never been.
Must I, wrongly condemned, for evermore
Endure the hate of him I wholly love ?
   He ordered me within the forest-grove
To dwell, in the earth-cave underneath the oak.
Ancient the earth-hall is, and, exiled here,
A longing unfulfilled consumes my life.
Dark are the valleys dim, and high the hills,   30
Bleak are my cavern-walls o'ergrown with briars,
Abode unblessed.   Alas, that e'er befell
My lord's far-faring !   The world holds many friends
Living in love, keeping the marriage-bed,
While at day-dawning all alone I go
In the earth-cavern underneath the oak !
I sit there through the lingering summer day,
There I beweep my wretched banishment,
The many miseries, sorrows of mind,
The yearnings vain this life has yielded me,
Haunting desires, from which I may not rest.   40
   Ever may that man, young in years, be sad ;
May his false smile belie his wretchedness ;
May his hard heart have cause of constant grief,
The torment of unrest ; may all his joy of life
Be shrunk within himself, be exiled there

In that far folk-land where now sits my friend
Under the cliffs of rock berimed with storm,
In dwelling drear, compassed with waters deep,
50 My heavy-hearted lover! Wretched is he;
His troubled mind recalls in thought too oft
A happier home. Alas, what woe is hers
Who waits with hopeless longing her beloved!

AURELIA I. HENRY.

GNOMIC VERSES

There are two sets of *Gnomic Verses*; sixty-six lines are preserved in the Cottonian manuscript, and two hundred and six lines in the *Exeter Book*.

The gnomes consist of proverbs, didactic and moral sentences, and simple reflections drawn from the observation of natural occurrences. It is often difficult to discover the reason for the order in which they appear, but the sequences often betray a genuine felicity, perhaps the product of a conscious art.

See Blanche C. Williams' edition of the verses (New York, 1914). Other works on the *Gnomic Verses* are Hugo Müller's dissertation, *Ueber die Angelsächsischen Versus Gnomici* (Jena, 1893), and Strobl's *Zur Spruchdichtung bei den Angelsachsen* (*Zeitschrift für Deutsche Philologie* **31** 54 ff.); cf. also Koegel's *Geschichte der Deutschen Litteratur* **1** 66 ff. The verses should be compared with the didactic poems, such as *The Father's Instruction*, with *Solomon and Saturn*, *Beowulf* (20 ff., 1002 ff., 1060 ff., 1384 ff., 2275 ff., 2764 ff.), and *The Seafarer*, Part II, p. 47.

(From the Cottonian MS.)

The sword shall lodge in the bosom, that noble iron.   25
The dragon shall dwell on the mound, old, and proud of
    his treasure.
The fish in the water shall bring forth his kind.
The king in his hall shall deal out gifts. . . .

Good striveth with evil; youth with age;   50
Life striveth with death; light with darkness;

Army fighteth with army.   Foe with foe
Throughout the land shall ever urge conflict.
Ever the wise man ponders the strife of this world.

The outlaw shall hang, justly pay for his crimes against
man.

Knoweth the Maker alone whither the soul shall fare—
All the spirits of men who fare to the Lord at the death-
day,[1]
60 And await, in the Father's keeping, their doom.
Dark and secret the future!
God alone knows it, our Father the Savior.
None shall come hither beneath these roofs
Who can riddle to men the Lord's creation —
The seats of the nations, the place of God's dwelling.

(From the Exeter Book.)

72 Frost shall freeze, fire melt wood.
The earth shall bloom.
Ice shall bridge the stream, a helm shall the water wear.
Wondrously spring the seeds of the earth.
One shall unbind the fetters of frost, e'en the Father
Almighty.
Winter shall wend away, fair weathers come again,
Summer be hot with its sun ; and restless be the sea. . . .

With beakers and armlets shall the king buy his queen ;
Both from the first shall be gracious with gifts.

[1] Cf. Bede's *Death-Song*, p. 78.

War-craft shall wax in the hero ; the wife shall thrive,
Dear to her people.   Blithe of mood shall she be,
Yet a keeper of secrets ; full generous too
In the giving of treasure and horses, in bestowing mead
    on the heroes.
Always, wherever it be, she greets the lord of the 90
    nobles,
Straightway bearing the first of the cups to the hand of
    her master.
They two who hold that house shall take counsel together.

The ship shall be nailed ; the shield shall be bound,
That light buckler of linden.

Dear to the Frisian wife is the one whom she welcomes,
When the vessel reaches the haven — his ship is at
    hand,
Her lord is come to his home, he who provideth for her,
And she summons him in ; she washes his sea-stained
    garments
And giveth him raiment new.   Full pleasant is it for 100
    him
Whose belovèd wife waiteth for him ashore !

                            CHAUNCEY B. TINKER.

RIDDLES

Nearly a hundred riddles, varying in length from one line to one hundred and seven lines, have been preserved, almost all of them being in the Exeter Book. Of these Wyatt in his edition says (pp. xxxii–xxxiii): 'By general agreement the *Riddles* belong, in the main, to the great period of OE. poetry, the 8th century. The folk-elements are no doubt earlier, and some of the folk-riddles may well be.' Editions are by Tupper (Boston, 1910) and Wyatt (Boston, 1912).

To some extent these English riddles are dependent — now more, now less — upon Latin predecessors, especially upon the hundred three-line riddles of Symphosius (perhaps sixth century), and the hundred of Aldhelm (639–709), having from four to eighty-three lines each. These have been edited, with verse translations, the former by Elizabeth H. du Bois (Woodstock, Vermont, 1912), the latter by James Hall Pitman (New Haven, 1925). Of the Old English ones, Stopford Brooke remarks (*English Literature . . . to the Norman Conquest*, p. 160): 'The best of them escape altogether from the Latin convention, and are English in matter and sentiment. . . . Those who state that these nobler *Riddles* are merely imitations are unable to distinguish between what is and what is not poetry.'

1. THE STORM–SPIRIT ON LAND

What hero's wit so dexterous and keen
Can tell who drives me onward in my course,
When in the terror of my strength I rise
Mid intermittent peals of thunder, hurtling,
Sweep over earth and smite with fire the buildings

70

Of nations, ravaging their halls ? The smoke
Tawny ascends above the roofs, and tumult
Is in the land, and men's death-agony.
Then I assail the woods, fair-fruited glades,
And fell the trees — I, canopied with water,   10
By powers sublime commissioned from afar
To drive in hurrying career. I wear
Upon my back that which enshrouded once
The habitants of earth of every kind,
Bodies and souls, within one common tomb.
Tell, now, what mighty power can compass me,
Or what I'm called, that can uplift this burden.

2. THE STORM–SPIRIT IN THE SEA

The billows crash above me while I move,
No man knows whither, searching out the earth
In the vast caverns of the sea. Then stirs
The ocean, and impels the watery mass
To burst in foam. Fiercely the whale-mere rises
And shouts aloud and groans in mighty pain,
While sounds the tramp of floods along the shore.
Against precipitous cliffs incessantly
Rocks, sand, and heaving waves and weeds are hurled.
Yet toiling, robed with the strength of many waters,
I stir the soil of ocean's ample grounds,   10
Nor can I 'scape the whelming tide, till he
That is my guide allows. O man of wisdom,
Tell who may wrest me from the encircling grasp
Of water, when the streams again are stilled,
And waves that covered me beat harmony.

7. THE SWAN

My robe is noiseless while I tread the earth,
Or tarry 'neath the banks, or stir the shallows ;
But when these shining wings, this depth of air,
Bear me aloft above the bending shores
Where men abide, and far the welkin's strength
Over the multitudes conveys me, then
With rushing whir and clear melodious sound
My raiment sings.   And like a wandering spirit
I float unweariedly o'er flood and field.

14. THE HORN

I was an armèd warrior, but now
The youthful courtier covers my proud neck
With twisted filigree of gold and silver.
Sometimes I 'm kissed by heroes, and again
I woo to battle with my melody
Comrades in full accord.   At times the courser
Bears me across the border, and again
Over the floods the stallion of the sea
Conveys me radiant with ornaments.
Sometimes a maiden, garlanded with jewels,
Brims full my winding bosom, and again
10 Perforce I lie — hard, headless, solitary
Upon the board.   Sometimes, set off with trappings,
In comely guise upon the wall I hang
Where heroes drink.   Again, horsed warriors
On forays wear me, glorious apparel ;
Then, dappled with gold, I must inspire the wind

From some one's bosom.   Whilom stately men
I summon to banquetings and wine ; sometimes
My voice resounds with freedom to the captive,
Flight to the foe.   Now find out what I 'm called.

23. THE BOW

My name is AGOB, with the letters changed.
I am a wondrous creature shaped for strife ;
When I am bent, and from my bosom darts
The venomous sting, with dexterous speed I send
Far and away the quivering stroke of death.
Soon as my guide who fashioned me for torture
Lets loose my pliant limbs, in agony
I stretch, until I vomit forth the broth
Of fatal, piercing poison that erewhile
I swallowed.   Never a man I then bespeak   10
Shall easily depart, once he is grazed
By that which takes its flight from out my vitals.
He makes dear purchase of the treacherous draught,
The full, stern cup which robs him of his life!
Except when fettered fast no use I serve ;
Unbound I fail.   Now tell what I am called.

26. THE BIBLE–CODEX

An enemy deprived me of my life,
Stripped me of worldly strength, immersed me then
In water, whence again he took me dripping,
Planted me in the sun, and there I lost
My nap of hair.   The knife's keen edge then dressed me,

Sharpened with pumice.   Fingers folded me,
And next the joyous quill traced eagerly
Across my burnished surface, scattering
The fluent drops along.   Again it drank
10 Of the tinctured stream, again stepped over me
With blackening print.   The craftsman bound me then
In leathern covers locked with golden clasps,
The wondrous work of artists.   Thus adorned
With scarlet dyes resplendent, lo! in me
The glorious abodes afar renowned,
The Shield of nations, and good will toward men!
    And if the children of this world will use me,
The happier, the surer of success
20 They 'll be, the keener-hearted, and in thought
The kinder, and more fraught with wisdom.   Then
More friends they 'll have — their own, familiar friends
So good and true, and capable, and trusty —
Who will prolong their fame and happiness
And hedge them round with graceful gifts, and fast
In bonds of love within their bosoms fold them.
Find out what I am called for men's advantage!
Famous in sacred story is my name,
Renowned 'mongst heroes, and itself divine.

27. THE MEAD

On every hand I 'm found and prized by men,
Borne from the fertile glades and castled heights
And vales and hills.   Daily the wings of bees
Carried me through the air, and with deft motion
Stored me beneath the low-crowned, sheltering roof.

Then in a cask men cherished me.   But now
The old churl I tangle, and trip, at last o'erthrow
Flat on the ground.   He that encounters me
And sets his will 'gainst my subduing might
Forthwith shall visit the earth upon his back!
If from his course so ill-advised he fails
To abstain, deprived of strength, yet strong in speech,
He's reft of all his power o'er hand or foot,
His mind dethroned.   Now find out what I'm called,
Who bind again the freeman to the soil,
Stupid from many a fall, in broad daylight!

79. THE FALCON

I'm bosom-friend to one of noble blood,
The soldier's comrade, minion of my lord,
And courtier to the king.   Sometimes on me
A fair-haired, stately woman lays her hand,
The queenliest daughter of a nobleman.
The bloom of the trees I wear upon my breast!
At times I ride perched on a fiery steed,
Leading the troop.   My tongue is dry and hard.
Oft when a seer sings his prophetic song,
I furnish fit reward.   Fine is my fashion,   10
And I am dark of hue.   Tell what I'm called.

HERBERT B. BROUGHAM.

III

RELIGIOUS LYRICS

CÆDMON'S HYMN

These verses probably form the first piece of extant English poetry composed on English soil, or at least they are the first that can be approximately dated. They are found at the end of the Moore manuscript of Bede's *Ecclesiastical History* in the University Library of Cambridge, England, and were probably copied there in or about the year 737. A facsimile of this inscription is in the Palæographical Society's *Facsimiles of Ancient Manuscripts*, Part IX, plate 140.

Cædmon's poetical activity falls within the abbacy of Hild of Whitby (658–680); this is all that we can know concerning the date, which may therefore fall not far from 665 or 670. The theme is praise to God as the Maker of heaven and earth for men, at once emphasizing the power, the eternity, and the beneficence of the Creator, together with the fact that all the marvels with which the universe is filled have proceeded from His hand. The substitution of the Hebraic cosmogony, and of this conception of divinity, for the pagan ones then current, of course wrought a profound change in the sentiments of the makers of English literature, and hence in the literature itself. How great was the influence of the new theory of creation may be gathered from the fact that it forms the theme of the minstrel's song in Hrothgar's hall (see p. 11), where the circumstances seem decidedly incongruous with it.

For the story of Cædmon, see Appendix, p. 180.

Now must we hymn the Master of heaven,
The might of the Maker, the deeds of the Father,
The thought of His heart.   He, Lord everlasting,
Established of old the source of all wonders :
Creator all-holy, He hung the bright heaven,
A roof high upreared, o'er the children of men ;
The King of mankind then created for mortals
The world in its beauty, the earth spread beneath them,
He, Lord everlasting, omnipotent God.

ALBERT S. COOK.

BEDE'S DEATH–SONG

The letter in which these lines occur was written by one of Bede's pupils, Cuthbert, to a fellow-student, Cuthwin, residing in a distant monastery, and describes the last hours of Bede's life. It is to be found in Mayor and Lumby's admirable edition of Books III and IV of the *Ecclesiastical History*, pp. 175–179, and in Plummer's edition of the *Ecclesiastical History*, I clx–clxiv. There are translations by Plummer, I lxxii–lxxviii, and by Tinker, in our *Select Translations from Old English Prose*, pp. 255–260. In the sentence introducing the lines, Bede is called 'learned in our songs.'

Before the dread journey which needs must be taken
No man is more mindful than meet is and right
To ponder, ere hence he departs, what his spirit
Shall, after the death-day, receive as its portion
Of good or of evil, by mandate of doom.

ALBERT S. COOK.

SELECTIONS FROM THE CHRIST

The *Christ* is one of four poems, containing in all 3838 lines, in which Cynewulf has inserted his name in runic characters —*Juliana, Elene, Christ,* and *Fates of the Apostles.* Concerning Cynewulf, the most acceptable view would seem to be that he was born about 705, and became Bishop of Lindisfarne in 740. This important see he held, according to an early twelfth-century chronicler, for a long time, 'though buffeted by the ever recurring blows of adverse circumstance.' In 750, when Offa, a son of King Aldfrith (see p. 9), had, after taking sanctuary at Lindisfarne, been dragged out and slain, Cynewulf, perhaps for having protected him, was imprisoned by the king to whom he owed his bishopric, and Frithobert, Bishop of Hexham, was installed in his place. Released after something like a year, Cynewulf resumed his office, and held it till 780, when, 'laying down worldly cares,' he voluntarily relinquished it to his successor, and died in 782 or 783 (Cook, *Trans. Conn. Acad.* 26 273–275).

The sources of the *Christ* are different for the three parts. For the First Part, *The Advent* (1–439), they consist of (1) the Greater Antiphons of Advent, sometimes called the O's; (2) four Antiphons included by certain mediæval churches among the Greater Antiphons, or associated with them; (3) two of the Antiphons for Lauds on Trinity Sunday according to the Sarum Use. For the Second Part, *The Ascension* (440–866), they consist of the close of Gregory the Great's homily on the Ascension, as contained in the Breviary under that season, and probably also of an Ascension hymn written by Bede. For the Third Part, *Doomsday* (867–1664), they consist (1) of the hymn 'Apparebit repentina,' etc., quoted by Bede, (2) of extracts from a sermon by Cæsarius of Arles (469–542), (3) of extracts from at least one sermon by Gregory the Great, besides minor passages from other works of that Father, and (4) probably of the account of Constantine's vision of the Cross, as related by Eusebius. For the discussion of these matters, and of Cynewulf as man and poet, see Cook's edition.

Selections 1 and 2 are from *The Advent;* 3–5 from *The Ascension;* the rest from *Doomsday*.

1. ANTIPHONAL PASSAGE

The suggestion for this passage is derived from the Antiphon of the Magnificat for December 21. This is, in the Latin:

'O Oriens, Splendor lucis æternæ, et Sol justitiæ: veni, et illumina sedentes in tenebris et umbra mortis;'

in the translation by Cardinal Newman:

'O Rising Brightness of the everlasting light and Sun of righteousness: come Thou and enlighten those who sit in darkness and in the shadow of death.'

Lo! Thou Splendor of the dayspring, fairest of angels sent to men upon earth, Thou Radiance of the Sun of righteousness, bright beyond the stars, Thou of Thy very self dost illumine all the tides of time! Even as Thou, God begotten of God, Son of the true Father,
110 didst ever dwell without beginning in the glory of heaven, so Thine own handiwork in its present need imploreth Thee with confidence that Thou send us the bright sun, and come in Thy very person to enlighten those who have long been covered with murky cloud, and sitting here in darkness and eternal night, shrouded in sins, have been forced to endure the shadow of death. Now in the fulness of hope we believe in the salvation
120 brought to men through the Word of God, who was in the beginning co-eternal with God the Father almighty, and afterward became flesh without blemish, being born of the virgin as a help for the afflicted. God appeared

among us without sin; the mighty Son of God and the
Son of Man dwelt together in harmony among mankind.
Wherefore it is right that we should ever give thanks by
our deeds unto the Lord of victory, for that He was
willing to send Himself unto us.

2. DIALOGUE BETWEEN MARY AND JOSEPH

This selection is especially interesting because of its dramatic
character.   Some scholars have even thought to find here the
origin of the English drama.

[*Mary*]. 'Alas my Joseph, son of Jacob, descendant
of the great king David, art thou bound to break off thy
firm troth and forsake my love?'

[*Joseph*]. 'I am full deeply troubled, bereft of my
good name; on thy account I have heard many words,
boundless causes of grief, taunts and contumely; they 170
utter insults and many reproaches against me.   Sad in
spirit I must needs pour out my tears.   God alone can
easily heal the sorrow of my heart and comfort me in
my misery.   Alas young damsel, maiden Mary!'

[*Mary*]. 'Why grievest thou and criest out in sorrow?
Never have I found in thee any fault, or cause for sus-
picion that thou hast wrought evil; and yet thou speakest
these words as if thou thyself wert filled with every sin 180
and iniquity.'

[*Joseph*]. 'I have endured too much misery because
of this child-bearing.   How can I refute their hateful
words, or find any answer to my enemies?   It is known
far and wide that from the glorious temple of the Lord
I willingly received a pure maiden free from sin, and now

all is changed by I know not what. Neither speech nor
190 silence avails me aught. If I declare the truth, then
must the daughter of David perish, slain with stones.
Yet is it harder for me to conceal crime ; as a perjurer
I should be forced to live thenceforth, hated of all peoples,
despised among the tribes of men.'

Then the maid unraveled the mystery, and thus she
spake : 'I swear truly by the Son of God, the Savior of
souls, that I have never yet had intercourse with any
200 man on earth ; but it was granted unto me, while yet
young in my home, that Gabriel, heaven's archangel,
bade me hail, and said in truth that the heavenly Spirit
would shine upon me with His splendor, and that I should
bear the Glory of life, an illustrious Child, the great Son
of God, the bright King of glory. Now without guilt
have I been made His temple ; the Spirit of comfort
hath dwelt within me. Do thou henceforth forego all
grievous care. Give eternal thanks unto God's great
Son that I have become His mother, though still a
210 maiden, and that thou art reputed His earthly father
in the thoughts of men ; thus was prophecy to be truly
fulfilled in Himself.'

3. THE ENDOWMENTS OF MANKIND

This selection should be compared with the poem, *The Gifts of
Men*. Reference should also be made to *The Fates of Men* (translated in Morley's *English Writers* 2 32 ff.).

Then He who created the earth, God's Spirit-son,
660 honored us and granted us gifts, eternal seats amid the
angels on high ; moreover He sowed manifold wisdom,

and planted it within the souls of men. Unto the mind
of one, through the Spirit of His mouth, He sendeth
wise eloquence and noble understanding; such a one
can sing and speak many things; unto his soul is com-
mitted the power of wisdom. One can awaken the harp
before warriors, touching it full loudly with his fingers. 670
One can set forth aright the law divine. One can tell
the course of the stars, the expanse of creation. One
can skilfully write the spoken word. To one He giveth
victory in war, when bowmen send the storm of darts,
the winged arrows, over their shields. One can boldly
urge forward his bark over the salt sea, and stir the
raging deep. One can climb the steep and lofty tree.
One can fashion the sword, the well-tempered weapon.
One knoweth the compass of the plains, the far-reaching 680
ways. So to us the Ruler, the Son of God, doth dis-
pense His gifts on earth. But to no man will He give
all wisdom of soul, lest, exalted above others by his own
power, his pride work him evil.

4. RUNE–PASSAGE

The large type denotes the runes of the original, which in succession spell the name of Cynewulf (in this poem, Cynwulf). These
renderings (following Gollancz in the main) are partly conjectural;
exactness, where that was possible, has been sacrificed in favor of
the proper initials. It would be more correct to substitute *bold* for
courageous, *misery* for *yearning*, *joy* for *winsomeness*, *sea* for *lake-
floods*, *wealth* for *fortune*. Cosijn regards the letters C, Y, and
N as forming *cyn* = 'mankind.' A similar rune-passage containing the poet's name will be found among the extracts from the
Elene (p. 141). Cynewulf has used the same device in his *Juliana*
and *Fates of the Apostles*.

Then shall the COURAGEOUS tremble; he shall hear
the King, the Ruler of heaven, speak stern words unto
those who in time past ill obeyed Him on earth, while
800 as yet they could easily find comfort for their YEARNING
and their NEED.   There in that place shall many a one,
weary and sore afraid, await what dire punishment He
will mete out to them for their deeds.   Gone is the
WINSOMENESS of earth's adornments.   Long ago the
portion of life's joys granted US was compassed about
by LAKE—FLOODS, our FORTUNE on the earth.   Then
shall our treasures burn in fire; bright and swift shall
the red flame rage; fiercely shall it rush through the
810 wide world.   Plains shall perish, citadels fall.   The fire
shall be all astir; pitilessly shall that greediest of spirits
waste the ancient treasure which men held of old, whilst
pride abode with them upon the earth.

5. LIFE COMPARED TO A VOYAGE

850   Now is it as though we fared in ships out upon the
ocean, over the waters cold, and urged our barks, our
sea-steeds, across the broad flood.   A perilous stream it
is, endless waves and wind-swept seas, on which we toss
throughout this fleeting world, over the fathomless reaches.
Hard was our life ere we sailed to land over the stormy
860 main.   Then came our help: God's Spirit-son guided us
to the haven of safety, and gave us grace to see, over the
vessel's side, where with firm-set anchor we should moor
our sea-steeds, those ocean-stallions old.   O let us fix our
hope in that holy haven above, which the Lord celestial
prepared for us when He ascended into the heavens!

6. DOOMSDAY

A favorite theme in Old English religious poetry. This extract is from the beginning of Part III. The beginning (stanzas A and C) of the alphabetical Latin hymn upon which it is based is thus translated by Calverley (*Works*, London, 1901, pp. 306–309):

As a thief who falls at midnight on his unsuspecting prey
When we think not shall o'ertake us the Almighty's Judgment Day.

.   .   .   .

Clanging over Earth's four quarters shall the sudden trumpet-call
Summon unto Christ's tribunal dead or living, one and all.

Lo! at midnight, unawares, the great day of the Lord omnipotent shall mightily overtake the dwellers on earth, the bright creation ; as oft a daring robber, a crafty 87c thief, prowling about in darkness, in the murky night, suddenly comes upon careless men bound in sleep, and sorely assails them unprepared.

Then together unto Mount Zion shall ascend a great multitude, radiant and joyful, the faithful of the Lord ; glory shall be theirs.   Thereupon from the four corners of the world, from the uttermost regions of earth, angels all-shining shall with one accord blow their crashing 880 trumpets ; the earth shall tremble under men.   Glorious and steadfast they shall sound together over against the course of the stars, chanting in harmony and making melody from south and from north, from east and from west, throughout the whole creation ; all mankind shall they wake from the dead unto the last judgment ; they shall rouse the sons of men all aghast from the ancient earth, bidding them straightway arise from their deep sleep.

There one may hear a sorrowing people, sad of heart
890 and greatly disquieted, sorely afraid and pitifully bewail-
ing the deeds done in the body. This shall be the
greatest forewarning ever shown unto men before or
since. There all the hosts of angels and of devils shall
mingle, the fair and the swart; there shall be a coming
of both the white and the black, according as an abode
is prepared all unlike for saints and sinners.

Then suddenly upon Mount Zion a blaze of the sun,
900 shining clear from the southeast, shall come forth from
the Creator, gleaming more brightly than the mind of
man can conceive, when the Son of God shall appear
hither through the vault of heaven. All glorious from
the eastern skies shall come the presence of Christ, the
aspect of the noble King, gentle in spirit toward His
own, bitter toward the wicked, wondrously varied, diverse
910 to the blessed and the forlorn. Unto the good, the host
of the holy, He shall be joyful of countenance, radiant,
winsome, loving, gracious, and fair. Sweet and pleasant
shall it be for His loved ones, for those who in days of
old pleased Him well by their words and deeds, to gaze
upon that shining face, winningly benign, upon the
advent of the King, the Lord of might. But unto the
evil and wicked, unto those who shall come to Him
undone by sin, He shall be terrible and awful to
920 behold.

That may be a prophetic intimation to him who is
wise of thought, that he shall have no cause whatever
to be afraid; he shall not be dismayed in soul at the
terror of the Presence, when he beholdeth the Lord of
all creation approaching with mighty wonders to the

doom of many, while on all sides press round Him a band of angels, a shining host, legions of the saints in great multitudes.

The vast creation shall resound, and the fiercest of raging fires shall sweep over the whole earth before the Lord; the fiery flame shall hurtle; the heavens shall burst asunder; all the firm-set flashing stars shall fall. The sun itself, which shone so brightly above the former world for the sons of men, shall be turned dark, even to the hue of blood; the moon, also, which of old gave light for mortals in the night season, shall fall headlong; and the stars shall be hurled from heaven by the fury of the storm-vexed air.

Now shall the Almighty, the glorious Prince, Creator of great kings, come into the assembly with His angel band.   An exultant host of His retainers shall be there also.   The souls of the blest shall journey with their Lord, when the Protector of men shall visit the nations of earth with dread punishment.   Then throughout the broad earth shall be heard the piercing blast of the heavenly trump; from seven quarters the winds shall rush, blowing and roaring with awful crash, rousing and blighting the world with storm, filling with terror the whole creation.   There shall be heard a deafening uproar, loud and violent, heavy and appalling, terrible unto mortals, of all tumults the mightiest. . . .

Thus shall the all-devouring spirit, the ravaging fire, overrun the earth and its lofty structures; the hot and greedy blast, famed afar, shall, over the earth's plain, fill the whole world with the terror of fire.   The city-walls shall fall in ruins.   Mountains shall melt away, along

with the headlands which erstwhile firm and steadfast
980 stoutly shielded the earth from ocean-floods, bulwarks
against the waves and heaving waters.   Then shall the
death-fire seize on every creature, both bird and beast;
the murky flame, a raging warrior, shall stride over the
earth.   Wheresoever the waters once flowed, the hurrying floods, there the fishes of the deep, cut off from
ocean, shall be consumed in a bath of fire; every sea-
monster exhausted shall die; water shall burn like wax.
There shall be more wonders than mind of man can
990 conceive — how whirlwind, and tempest, and raging
blast shall rend the broad creation.   Men shall wail;
they shall weep and lament with mournful voices, down-
cast and wretched, overwhelmed with sorrow.   The
swart flame shall blaze on those fordone by sin; the
fire shall consume the golden ornaments, all the ancient
treasure of the kings of the nations.   There amid the
sounds from heaven an outcry shall be heard, wailing
and lamentation, the strife of the living, loud weeping,
1000 and the sad plaint of men.   Herefrom no man guilty of
crime can win refuge, or anywhere escape from the
flame, but that fire shall seize on all things throughout
the earth; it shall fiercely delve and eagerly explore the
regions of the world within and without, until the glowing flame hath wholly purged away by its billowing the
stain of earthly sin.

Then in great majesty shall God almighty come to
that dread mount; the holy King of heavenly angels,
1010 the Lord omnipotent, shall shine resplendent upon the
multitudes; round about Him shall brightly gleam a
most goodly throng, holy bands, the blessed company of

angels ; with terror of the Father shall they tremble,
dismayed in their inmost thoughts.   Wherefore it is no
marvel that the unclean race of men should greatly fear
and pitifully lament, since even the holy race, the white
host of archangels, heaven-bright, are sore affrighted
before that Presence, what time the radiant beings await 1020
with trembling the judgment of the Lord.   Most terrible
of all days shall that be in the world when the King of
glory shall chasten all peoples by His might, and bid
speech-uttering men, tribe after tribe, arise from their
graves and come every one unto the assembly.

7. THE APPARITION OF THE ROOD

A large part of the Old English poetry on the Cross has been
gathered in the pages following (93–103).

There shall sinful men, sad at heart, behold the greatest
affliction.   Not for their behoof shall the cross of our
Lord, brightest of beacons, stand before all nations, wet
with the pure blood of heaven's King, stained with His
gore, shining brightly over the vast creation.   Shadows
shall be put to flight when the resplendent cross shall
blaze upon all peoples.   But this shall be for an affliction 1090
and a punishment to men, to those malefactors who knew
no gratitude to God, that He, the King, was crucified
on the holy rood for the sins of mankind, on that day
when He whose body knew no sin nor base iniquity
lovingly purchased life for men with the price with which
He ransomed us.   For all this will He rigorously exact 1100
recompense when the red rood shall shine brightly over
all in the sun's stead.

Fearfully and sorrowfully shall they look thereon, those black workers of iniquity, fordone by sin ; they shall behold to their bale that which would have been their greatest weal, had they been willing to apprehend it as their good.   With sad hearts shall they behold the ancient gashes and open wounds upon their Lord, where

1110 His foes pierced with nails the white hands and the holy feet, and let forth gore from His side ; blood and water gushed forth together before the eyes of all the people, when He was on the cross.   All this they themselves shall then be able to see, open and manifest, how He suffered many things for the love of sinners.   The sons of men shall clearly behold how the false-hearted denied Him,

1120 mocked Him with blasphemies, spat their spittle in His face, and spake insults against Him ; how hell-doomed men, blind of thought, foolish and erring, struck that blessed countenance with their hands, with their out-stretched palms, with their very fists, and round His head entwined a cruel crown of thorns.

They saw that the dumb creation — verdant earth and high heaven — shudderingly felt the sufferings of their

1130 Lord ; and though they had not life, yet moaned in sorrow when wicked men seized on their Savior with impious hands.   The sun became darkened, obscured by misery. . . .

Trees likewise many, and by no means few, declared

1170 who had shaped them with their branches, when almighty God ascended one of them and suffered pain for men's weal, loathsome death for the help of mankind.   Then was many a tree suffused with bloody tears beneath its bark, red and frequent ; the sap turned to gore.

8. FROM THE ADDRESS OF THE SAVIOUR AT THE LAST JUDGMENT

'How unequal was the reckoning betwixt us two! I bore thy pain that thou, happy and blessed, mightst 1460 possess my kingdom ; and by my death I dearly bought long life for thee, that thenceforth thou mightst dwell in light, radiant and free from sin. My body, which had harmed no man, lay buried in the earth, hidden beneath in the tomb, that thou mightst dwell in splendor in the skies above, mighty amid the angels.'

9. THE JOYS OF THE BLESSED

But the elect shall bring before Christ bright treasures ; their glory shall live at the judgment day; they shall possess the joy of a tranquil life with God, such as is granted unto every saint in the kingdom of heaven. That is the home which shall have no end, and there for evermore the sinless shall possess their joy, and, 1640 clothed with light, enfolded in peace, shielded from sorrows, honored by joys, endeared to the Savior, shall praise the Lord, the beloved Protector of life ; radiant with grace they shall enjoy in bliss the fellowship of angels, and worship the Guardian of men for ever and ever. The Father of all shall have and hold dominion over the hosts of the sanctified.

There is song of angels, joy of the blest ; there is the dear presence of the Lord, brighter than the sun unto 1650 the blessèd ; there is the love of dear ones ; life without death ; a joyous multitude of men ; youth without age ;

the glory of the heavenly hosts ; health without pain ;
rest without toil for the workers of righteousness ; bliss
of the happy ; day without darkness, bright and glad-
some ; happiness without sorrow ; harmony without strife
'twixt friends rejoicing in heaven ; peace without enmity
1660 in the congregation of the saints.   No hunger shall be
there, nor thirst, nor sleep, nor sore disease, nor scorch-
ing of the sun, nor cold, nor care ; but there the company of the blest, most radiant of hosts, shall for ay
enjoy the grace of their King and glory with their
Lord.

CHARLES H. WHITMAN.

THE DREAM OF THE ROOD

The date and authorship of this poem are unknown. It probably belongs to a period at least as late as that of Cynewulf, and may possibly be from his hand. Special interest attaches to it because of its relation to the runic inscription on the Ruthwell Cross, for which see p. 100.

The cross of the opening lines was probably suggested by the vision of Constantine, while Helena's Invention of the Cross is reflected in lines 75 ff., which recall Cynewulf's *Elene*. The latter half of the poem has several points of contact with the *Christ*.

The last paragraph seems like an inartistic addition.

For a discussion of the poem in various aspects, see Cook's edition (Oxford and New York, 1905).

Hark! of a matchless vision would I speak,
Which once I dreamed at midnight, when mankind
At rest were dwelling. Then methought I saw
A wondrous cross extending up on high,
With light encircled, tree of trees most bright.
That beacon all was overlaid with gold;
And near the earth stood precious stones ablaze,
While five more sparkled on the shoulder-beam.
Gazing on it were angels of the Lord,
From their first being's dawn all beautiful.
No cross was that of wickedness and shame,   10
But holy spirits, men on earth, and all
The glorious creation on it gazed.

Sublime the tree victorious ; while I,
Stained with iniquity, was galled with sins.
There, clothed as with a garment, I beheld
That tree of glory shining joyfully,
Adorned with gold, enriched with precious stones,
Which covered worthily the Ruler's cross.
However, through the gold I could perceive
That wretched ones had battled there of old ;
For on the right side once it had been bleeding.
20 Then all my spirit was with sorrow stirred ;
Fearful was I before that radiant sight.
There I beheld that beacon, quick to change,
Alter in vesture and in coloring ;
Now dewed with moisture, soiled with streaming blood,
And now with gold and glittering gems adorned.
A long time lying there I sadly looked
Upon the Savior's cross, until I heard
Resounding thence a voice.   That wood divine
Then spake these words :
       ' It was long, long ago —
Yet I recall — when, at the forest's edge,
I was hewn down, and from my stem removed.
30 Resistless were the foes that seized me there,
They fashioned for themselves a spectacle,
Commanded me to bear their criminals ;
And on men's shoulders carried me away
Until they set me down upon a hill,
And stayed me fast ; mine enemies indeed !
' Then I beheld the Master of mankind
Approach with lordly courage as if He
Would mount upon me, and I dared not bow

Nor break, opposing the command of God,
Although I saw earth tremble ; all my foes
I might have beaten down, yet I stood fast.
    ' Then the young Hero laid His garments by,
He that was God almighty, strong and brave ;
And boldly in the sight of all He mounted   40
The lofty cross, for He would free mankind.
Then, as the Man divine clasped me, I shook ;
Yet dared I not bow to the earth nor fall
Upon the ground, but I must needs stand fast.
    ' A cross upraised, I lifted a great King,
Lifted the Lord of heaven ; and dared not bow.
    ' They pierced me with dark nails, and visible
Upon me still are scars, wide wounds of malice,
Yet might I injure none among them all.
They mocked us both together ; then was I
All wet with blood, which streamed from this Man's side
When He at length had breathed His spirit out.
    ' Many a vile deed I suffered on that mount ;   50
The God of hosts I saw harshly outstretched,
And darkness hid the body of the King,
With clouds enshrouded its effulgent light ;
Forth went a shadow, black beneath the clouds ;
And all creation wept, lamented long —
Their King had fallen, Christ was on the cross.
    ' Yet eagerly some hastened from afar
To Him who was their Prince ; all this I saw.
Ah, then with sorrow was I deeply stirred ;
Yet to the hand of men I bowed me down,
Humbly, with ardent zeal.   They took Him then,   60
Lifted from His dire pain almighty God.

The warriors left me standing, swathed in blood,
And with sharp arrows wounded sore was I.
Him they laid gently down, weary of limb,
And stood beside His body at the head,
Gazing upon the Lord of heaven ; while He
Rested a while, with His great labor spent.
Then in the slayers' sight men there began
To build a sepulchre, from marble hewn ;
And laid therein the Lord of victories.
A song of sorrow then for Him they sang,
The desolate at eventide, when they,
O'erwearied, would depart from their great King.
And so companionless He rested.
                                    'We,
70   After the warriors' cry uprose, yet stood
A long while there, on our foundations dripping.
The corpse, fair dwelling of the soul, grew cold.
    'Then one began to fell us to the earth —
A fearful fate! and in the entombing mold
Deep buried us.   Yet, undismayed, for me
The friends and followers of the Lord made search —
And when from out the earth they lifted me,
With silver they adorned me, and with gold.
    'Now mayest thou know, O hero mine, beloved!
Unutterable sorrows I endured,
80   Base felons' work.   But now hath come the time
When, far and wide, men on the earth, and all
The glorious universe doth honor me,
And to this beacon bow themselves in prayer.
On me a while suffered the Son of God ;
Therefore now full of majesty I tower

High under heaven ; and I have power to heal
All those who do me reverence.
                              ' Of old
Was I a punishment, the cruelest,
The most abhorred by men, ere I for man
Had opened the true way of life.   Lo, then
The Prince of glory, Guardian of heaven,   90
Above all other trees exalted me,
As He, almighty God, in sight of men
His mother honored, blessèd among women,
Mary herself.
                  ' Now, hero mine, beloved,
I bid thee tell this vision unto men,
Reveal with words that 'tis the glory-tree
On which almighty God suffered for sin,
The many sins of man, and Adam's deeds
Done long ago.   There once He tasted death ;   100
But afterwards the Lord from death arose
By His own mighty power, a help for men.
To heaven He then ascended, whence shall come
Once more upon the earth to seek mankind
At the last judgment day, the Lord himself,
Almighty God, surrounded by His angels.
And there shall He, who hath the power of doom,
Adjudge to every one the just reward
Which he on earth, in this short life, hath earned.
Then unabashed and bold can no one be   110
Before the word which He, the Ruler, speaks :
" Where is the man," He asks the multitude,
"Who for the Lord would taste of bitter death
As He Himself once did upon the cross ? "

Then are they fearful, little can devise
What they shall say to Christ.   But need is none
That any at that time should be afraid
Who beareth in his heart this sacred sign ;
For through the cross alone must every soul
120   Seek out the Kingdom from the earthly way,
Who hopes hereafter with the King to dwell.'

Happy in mind I prayed then to the rood
With great devotion, where I was alone
Without companionship ; my soul within
Was quickened to depart, so many years
Of utter weariness had I delayed.
And now my life's great happiness is this,
That to the cross victorious I may come
Alone, above the wont of other men,
To worship worthily.   Desire for this
130   Is great within my heart, and all my help
Must reach me from the rood.   Of powerful friends
Not many do I own on earth, for hence
Have they departed, from the world's delights ;
They followed after Him, their glorious King,
And with the Father now in heaven they live,
Dwelling in bliss.   Each day I longing ask :
'When will the cross of Christ, which formerly
I here on earth beheld, call me away
From this my transient life, and bring me hence
To all delight, the joyous harmonies
140   Of heaven, where sit at feast the folk of God,
And gladness knows no end — so placing me
Where with the saints in glory I may dwell,

Enjoying greatly their glad minstrelsy?'
Be gracious unto me, O Lord, who once
For sins of men suffered upon the cross.
He freed us, gave us life, and home in heaven.

Hope was restored with blessedness and joy
To those who had erewhile endured the fire.
Triumphant in this journey was the Son,   150
Mighty and prosperous, when He advanced
Into God's kingdom with a multitude,
A host of souls; when to His angels came
The almighty Master for their joy, to those
The holy ones in heaven, who from the first
Had dwelt in glory; when their Ruler came,
Almighty God, into His fatherland.

LAMOTTE IDDINGS.

RUTHWELL CROSS INSCRIPTION

The following description is slightly condensed from Anderson, *Scotland in Early Times*, Second Series, pp. 232 ff.: ' At Ruthwell, in Annandale, within eight miles of Dumfries, there stands a very remarkable monument. Its form is that of a tall free-standing cross. As it stands at present, the cross is reconstructed. The whole height of the cross is about seventeen and a half feet, the shaft being two feet in breadth at the base, and fifteen inches in thickness. The material is sandstone. It stood in the old church of Ruthwell till 1642, when the General Assembly which met at St. Andrews on 27th July of that year issued an order for its destruction as a monument of idolatry. The transverse arms are still wanting, those now on the monument having been supplied in 1823. The monument is sculptured with figure-subjects on the broad faces, and on its sides with scroll-work. The figure-subjects on the broad faces of the cross are arranged in panels surrounded with flat borders, on which are incised the inscriptions which give to this monument its special interest. They are in two languages and two alphabets, one set being carved in Roman capitals, the other in runes. The runes are on the raised borders enclosing the two panels of scroll-work, and are arranged in vertical columns, extending from top to bottom, with the exception of the first line, which runs horizontally across the top of the panel. Consequently it reads from left to right across the first line, in the usual way, then continues in a vertical line down the whole of the right-hand border, returning to the top of the left-hand border, and reading vertically again to the base. As the lower part of the cross is more wasted than the upper, there are places where the reading fails toward the bottom of each border, thus making four gaps in the continuity of the inscription.'

Nos. I and II below represent respectively the right- and the left-hand inscriptions of the one face; III and IV the right- and the left-hand ones of the opposite face. The three words, 'Christ was on,' represent the horizontal line referred to above. All, it should be said, are below the transverse arms of the cross. It has often been affirmed, but, as now appears, without any sufficient reason, that Cædmon recorded his name upon the cross as the maker, and hence that he is to be credited with the authorship of the poem whose fragments are translated below — fragments whose striking correspondence with portions of the *Dream of the Rood* was first pointed out by Kemble in 1843. By many scholars it has been supposed that the inscription on the cross belongs to the seventh or eighth century, but there are good grounds for believing that it is rather to be dated about the year 1150, and that it was erected at the command or under the influence of David I of Scotland, who ruled over Scottish Cumbria, the region including Ruthwell, from 1107 to 1153, who founded various monasteries, and who was in a position to command the services of accomplished architects and sculptors. For the history of opinion on the subject, reasons for favoring the later date, and photographs of this and the Bewcastle Cross, see Cook, *The Date of the Ruthwell and Bewcastle Crosses* (New Haven, 1912).

The inscription should be compared with *Dream of the Rood* 38 ff.

I

(Un)clothed Himself God almighty when He would mount the cross, courageous in the sight of all men; bow . . . .

II

. . . I the powerful King, the Lord of heaven; I durst not bend. Men mocked us both together. I was bedewed with blood, shed from . . . .

III

Christ was on the rood. But hastening thither came noble ones from afar to the One (*or*, to the solitary One); all that I beheld. Grievously was I afflicted with sorrows; bowed . . . .

IV

. . . wounded with arrows. They laid Him down, weary of limb, stood at His body's head; beheld Him there heaven . . . .

ALBERT S. COOK.

BRUSSELS CROSS INSCRIPTION

This inscription is found upon a reliquary said to contain fragments of the true cross, preserved in the Cathedral of Brussels. According to Logeman, who first published and correctly translated the inscription, it dates from about the year 1100, as nearly as he can judge; Cook (*Modern Language Review* **10** 159, April, 1915) would assign it to about 1040. Besides the verses, it has this statement: 'Æthelmær and Æthelwold his brother caused this cross to be made to the glory of Christ, for the soul of Ælfric their brother. Drahmal wrought me.' For the persons mentioned, see the article referred to above. The lines translated below are closely related to ll. 42, 44, 48 of the *Dream of the Rood*, and are probably adapted from that poem, like those on the Ruthwell Cross (see p. 100). Full details concerning the reliquary may be found in Logeman's brochure, *L'Inscription Anglo-Saxonne du Reliquaire de la Vraie Croix*, Ghent and Leipzig, 1891.

Rood is my name.   Once long ago I bore
Trembling, bedewed with blood, the mighty King.

CHAUNCEY B. TINKER.

IV

BIBLICAL POEMS

SELECTIONS FROM THE GENESIS

Genesis, Exodus, Daniel, and *Christ and Satan,* the so-called Cædmonian poems, were first published by Franciscus Junius at Amsterdam in 1655. By reason of the resemblance which their subjects bore to those of the poems described by Bede (see Appendix, p. 180), Junius conjectured that the entire series was the work of Cædmon. Modern scholarship has, however, concluded that no part of the poems can safely be attributed to Cædmon. Discrepancies of language, metre, and style seem to make impossible the attribution of the series to any one man. Wülker, for example, assigns the *Exodus,* the *Daniel,* and the older part of the *Genesis* to the first half of the eighth century (*Geschichte der Englischen Litteratur,* p. 35); Clubb, in his edition (New Haven, 1925), would date the *Christ and Satan* between 790 and 830.

The *Genesis* falls into two parts, *Genesis A* and *Genesis B.* The latter comprises lines 235–851, and probably belongs to some period of the tenth century; the former includes the rest of the poem. Up to 1875 the whole was supposed to be the work of the same author, but in that year Sievers (*Der Heliand und die Angelsächsische Genesis,* Halle, 1875) made the brilliant discovery that lines 235–851 were an insertion, and that they were a translation from Old Saxon. In 1894 this hypothesis, which had been generally accepted on the basis of the internal evidence adduced by Sievers, was strikingly confirmed by the discovery in a Vatican manuscript of certain fragments of an Old Saxon *Genesis,*

twenty-six lines of which correspond with a part of *Genesis B* (cf.
Zangemeister and Braune, *Bruchstücke der Altsächsischen Bibeldichtung*, Heidelberg, 1894; Piper, *Die Altsächsische Bibeldichtung* I, Stuttgart, 1897). Sievers at first supposed that the original of
Genesis B was by the author of the Old Saxon *Heliand* (about 830);
he now believes (*Zeitschrift für Deutsche Philologie* **27** 538) that
the fragments are the work of a pupil and successor of the *Heliand*-
poet, while Kögel (*Geschichte der Deutschen Litteratur* **1** 280,
288 c) and Braune (*Bruchstücke* 35), for example, believe that the
poet first wrote the *Heliand*, and afterward the *Genesis*, as Sievers
had already suspected in 1878 (*Heliand*, p. xxxiv). The relation between the Old Saxon original and the Old English is
exhibited in the Appendix (pp. 184–185), where the only extant
fragment of the original which corresponds to a passage of *Genesis
B* is printed side by side with this passage. In some parts of
Genesis B the adaptation of the Old Saxon original by the Old
English poet is undoubtedly characterized by greater freedom
than is shown in the passage just referred to.

The selections which follow are of especial interest because of
their similarity to certain parts of *Paradise Lost*. The following
parallels are especially noteworthy: *Gen.* 32 and *P. L.* 5. 688–689;
Gen. 337 and *P. L.* 1. 84 ff.; *Gen.* 356 ff. and *P. L.* 1. 242 ff.;
Gen. 395 ff. and *P. L.* 1. 650 ff., 2. 345–376; *Gen.* 449 and *P. L.* 1.
222–224. It is not impossible that Milton may have been
acquainted with the *Genesis;* Masson (*Life of Milton* **6** 557, note)
regards it as possible, but Wülker (*Anglia* **4** 401 ff.) considers it
unlikely; cf. Cook, ' Milton and Cædmon,' *Academy* **34** 420.

After the present selections, the Biblical paraphrase is continued
as far as the Sacrifice of Isaac.

GENESIS A

1. THE FALL OF THE ANGELS

Most right it is that we praise with our words,
Love in our minds, the Warden of the skies,

Glorious King of all the hosts of men;
He speeds the strong, and is the Head of all
His high creation, the almighty Lord.
None formed Him, no first was nor last shall be
Of the eternal Ruler, but His sway
Is everlasting over thrones in heaven.
    With powers on high, soothfast and steadfast, He
10 Ruled the wide home of heaven's bosom spread
By God's might for the guardians of souls,
The sons of glory.   Hosts of angels shone,
Glad with their Maker; bright their bliss, and rich
The fruitage of their lives; their glory sure,
They served and praised their King, with joy gave praise
To Him, their Life-lord, in whose aiding care
They judged themselves most blessèd.
                                    Sin unknown,
20 Offense unformed, still with their Parent-Lord
They lived in peace, raising aloft in heaven
Right and truth only, ere the angel-chief
Through pride divided them and led astray.
Their own well-being they would bear no more,
But cast themselves out of the love of God.
Great in presumption against the Most High,
They would divide the radiant throng far spread,
The resting-place of glory.   Even there
Pain came to them; envy and pride began
30 There first to weave ill counsel, and to stir
The minds of angels.   Then, athirst for strife,
He said that northward he would own in heaven
A home and a high throne.   Then God was wroth,
And for the host He had made glorious,

For those pledge-breakers, our souls' guardians,
The Lord made anguish a reward, a home
In banishment, hell-groans, hard pain, and bade
That torture-house abide their joyless fall.   40
When with eternal night and sulphur-pains,
Fulness of fire, dread cold, reek and red flames,
He knew it filled, then through that hopeless home
He bade the woeful horror to increase.
Banded in blameful counsel against God,
Their wrath had wrath for wages.   In fierce mood
They said they would, and might with ease, possess
The kingdom.   Him that lying hope betrayed,
After the Lord of might, high King of heaven,   50
Highest, upraised His hand against that host.
False and devoid of counsel, they might not
Share strength against their Maker.   He in wrath
Clave their bold mood, bowed utterly their boast,
Struck from the sinful scathers kingdom, power,
Glory, and gladness: from the opposers took
His joy, His peace, their bright supremacy,
And, with sure march, by His own might poured down
Avenging anger on His enemies.   60
Stern in displeasure, with consuming wrath,
By hostile grasp He crushed them in His arms;
Ireful He from their home, their glory-seats
Banished His foes; and that proud angel-tribe,
Malicious host of spirits bowed with care,
He, the Creator, Lord of all might, sent
Far journeying, with bruised pride and broken threat,
Strength bent, and beauty blotted.   They, exiled,   70
Were bound on their swart ways.   Loud laugh no more

Was theirs, but in hell-pain they wailed accursed,
Knowing sore sorrow and the sulphur-throes,
Roofed in with darkness: the full recompense
Of those advancing battle against God.

2. The Beginning of Creation

But after as before was peace in Heaven,
Fair rule of love; dear unto all the Lord
80   Of lords, the King of hosts, to all His own,
And glories of the good who possessed joy
In heaven the almighty Father still increased.
Then peace was among dwellers in the sky,
Blaming and lawless malice were gone out,
And angels feared no more, since plotting foes
Who cast off heaven were bereft of light.
Their glory-seats behind them in God's realm,
Enlarged with gifts, stood happy, bright with bloom,
90   But ownerless since the cursed spirits went
Wretched to exile within bars of hell.
    Then thought within His mind the Lord of hosts
How He again might fix within His rule
The great creation, thrones of heavenly light
High in the heavens for a better band,
Since the proud scathers had relinquished them.
The holy God, therefore, in His great might
Willed that there should be set beneath heaven's span
100   Earth, firmament, wide waves, created world,
Replacing foes cast headlong from their home.
Here yet was naught save darkness of the cave,
The broad abyss, whereon the steadfast King

Looked with His eyes and saw that space of gloom,
Saw the dark cloud lower in lasting night,
Was deep and dim, vain, useless, strange to God,
Black under heaven, wan, waste, till through His word 110
The King of glory had created life.
   Here first the eternal Father, guard of all,
Of heaven and earth, raised up the firmament,
The almighty Lord set firm by His strong power
This roomy land; grass greened not yet the plain,
Ocean far spread hid the wan ways in gloom.
Then was the Spirit gloriously bright
Of heaven's Keeper borne over the deep   120
Swiftly.   The Life-giver, the angel's Lord,
Over the ample ground bade come forth light.
Quickly the high King's bidding was obeyed,
Over the waste there shone light's holy ray.
Then parted He, Lord of triumphant might,
Shadow from shining, darkness from the light.
Light, by the word of God, was first named day.   130

GENESIS B

1. The Fall of Satan

The Almighty had disposed ten angel-tribes,
The holy Father by His strength of hand,
That they whom He well trusted should serve Him
And work His will.   For that the holy God   250
Gave intellect, and shaped them with His hands.
In happiness He placed them, and to one
He added prevalence and might of thought,

Sway over much, next highest to Himself
In heaven's realm.   Him He had wrought so bright
That pure as starlight was in heaven the form
Which God the Lord of hosts had given him.
Praise to the Lord his work, and cherishing
Of heavenly joy, and thankfulness to God
For his share of that gift of light, which then
Had long been his.   But he perverted it,
Against heaven's highest Lord he lifted war,
260   Against the Most High in His sanctuary.
Dear was he to our Lord, but was not hid
From Him that in His angel pride arose.
He raised himself against his Maker, sought
Speech full of hate and bold presuming boast,
Refused God suit, said that his own form beamed
With radiance of light, shone bright of hue,
And in his mind he found not service due
To the Lord God, for to himself he seemed
270   In force and skill greater than all God's host.
Much spake the angel of presumption, thought
Through his own craft to make a stronger throne
Higher in heaven.   His mind urged him, he said,
That north and south he should begin to work,
Found buildings; said he questioned whether he
Would serve God. 'Wherefore,' he said, 'shall I toil?
No need have I of master.   I can work
280   With my own hands great marvels, and have power
To build a throne more worthy of a God,
Higher in heaven.   Why shall I for His smile
Serve Him, bend to Him thus in vassalage?
I may be God as He.

Stand by me, strong supporters firm in strife.
Hard-mooded heroes, famous warriors,
Have chosen me for chief; one may take thought
With such for counsel, and with such secure
Large following.   My friends in earnest they,
Faithful in all the shaping of their minds;
I am their master, and may rule this realm.
Therefore it seems not right that I should cringe   290
To God for any good, and I will be
No more His servant.'
                    When the Almighty heard
With how great pride His angel raised himself
Against his Lord, foolishly spake high words
Against the supreme Father, he that deed
Must expiate, and in the work of strife
Receive his portion, take for punishment
Utmost perdition.   So doth every man
Who sets himself in battle against God,
In sinful strife against the Lord most high.
Then was the Mighty wroth, heaven's highest Lord   300
Cast him from his high seat, for he had brought
His Master's hate on him.   His favor lost,
The Good was angered against him, and he
Must therefore seek the depth of hell's fierce pains,
Because he strove against heaven's highest Lord,
Who shook him from His favor, cast him down
To the deep dales of hell, where he became
Devil.   The fiend with all his comrades fell
From heaven, angels, for three nights and days,
From heaven to hell, where the Lord changed them all
To devils, because they His deed and word

310 Refused to worship.   Therefore in worse light
Under the earth beneath, almighty God
Had placed them triumphless in the swart hell.
   There evening, immeasurably long,
Brings to each fiend renewal of the fire ;
Then comes, at dawn, the east wind keen with frost ;
Its dart, or fire continual, torment sharp,
The punishment wrought for them, they must bear.
Their world was changed, and those first times filled
   hell
320 With the deniers.   Still the angels held,
They who fulfilled God's pleasure, heaven's heights ;
Those others, hostile, who such strife had raised
Against their Lord, lie in the fire, bear pangs,
Fierce burning heat in midst of hell, broad flames,
Fire and therewith also the bitter reek
Of smoke and darkness ; for they paid no heed
To service of their God ; their wantonness
Of angel's pride deceived them, who refused
To worship the almighty Word.   Their pain
330 Was great, then were they fallen to the depth
Of fire in the hot hell for their loose thought
And pride unmeasured, sought another land
That was without light and was full of flame,
Terror immense of fire.   Then the fiends felt
That they unnumbered pains had in return,
Through might of God, for their great violence,
But most for pride.

2. Satan's Address to his Followers

Then spoke the haughty king,
Once brightest among angels, in the heavens
Whitest, and to his Master dear beloved
Of God until they lightly went astray,   340
And for that madness the almighty God
Was wroth with him and into ruin cast
Him down to his new bed, and shaped him then
A name, said that the highest should be called
Satan thenceforth, and o'er hell's swart abyss
Bade him have rule and avoid strife with God.
Satan discoursed, he who henceforth ruled hell
Spake sorrowing.
God's angel erst, he had shone white in heaven,   350
Till his soul urged, and most of all its pride,
That of the Lord of hosts he should no more
Bend to the Word.   About his heart his soul
Tumultuously heaved, hot pains of wrath
Without him.
     Then said he : 'Most unlike this narrow place
To that which once we knew, high in heaven's realm,
Which my Lord gave me, though therein no more
For the Almighty we hold royalties.   360
Yet right hath He not done in striking us
Down to the fiery bottom of hot hell,
Banished from heaven's kingdom, with decree
That He will set in it the race of man.
Worst of my sorrows this, that, wrought of earth,
Adam shall sit in bliss on my strong throne,
Whilst we these pangs endure, this grief in hell.

Woe! Woe! had I the power of my hands,
And for a season, for one winter's space,
370   Might be without; then with this host I —
But iron binds me round; this coil of chains
Rides me; I rule no more; close bonds of hell
Hem me their prisoner.   Above, below,
Here is vast fire, and never have I seen
More loathly landscape; never fade the flames,
Hot over hell.   Rings clasp me, smooth hard bands
Mar motion, stay my wandering — feet bound,
380   Hands fastened, and the ways of these hell-gates
Accursed so that I cannot free my limbs;
Great lattice-bars, hard iron hammered hot,
Lie round me, wherewith God hath bound me down
Fast by the neck.
                           ' So know I that He knew
My mind, and that the Lord of hosts perceived
That if between us two by Adam came
Evil towards that royalty of heaven,
I having power of my hands —
But now we suffer throes in hell, gloom, heat,
390   Grim, bottomless; us God Himself hath swept
Into these mists of darkness, wherefore sin
Can He not lay against us that we planned
Evil against Him in the land.   Of light
He hath shorn us, cast us into utmost pain.
May we not then plan vengeance, pay Him back
With any hurt, since shorn by Him of light?
Now He hath set the bounds of a mid-earth
Where after His own image He hath wrought
Man, by whom He will people once again

Heaven's kingdom with pure souls.   Therefore intent
Must be our thought that, if we ever may,
On Adam and his offspring we may wreak
Revenge, and, if we can devise a way,   400
Pervert His will.   I trust no more the light
Which he thinks long to enjoy with angel-power.
Bliss we obtain no more, nor can attain
To weaken God's strong will ; but let us now
Turn from the race of man that heavenly realm
Which may no more be ours, contrive that they
Forfeit His favor, undo what His word
Ordained ; then wroth of mind He from His grace
Will cast them, then shall they too seek this hell
And these grim depths.   Then may we for ourselves
Have them in this strong durance, sons of men
For servants.   Of the warfare let us now
Begin to take thought.   If of old I gave
To any thane, while we in that good realm   410
Sat happy and had power of our thrones,
Gifts of a prince, then at no dearer time
Could he reward my gift, if any now
Among my followers would be my friend,
That he might pass forth upward from these bounds,
Had power with him that, winged, he might fly,
Borne on the clouds, to where stand Adam and Eve
Wrought on earth's kingdom, girt with happiness,   420
While we are cast down into this deep dale.
Now these are worthier to the Lord, may own
The blessing rightly ours in heaven's realm,
This the design apportioned to mankind.
Sore is my mind and rue is in my thought

That ever henceforth they should possess heaven.
If ever any of you in any way
May turn them from the teaching of God's word,
They shall be evil to Him, and if they
430 Break His commandment, then will He be wroth
Against them, then will be withdrawn from them
Their happiness, and punishment prepared,
Some grievous share of harm.   Think all of this,
How to deceive them.   In these fetters then
I can take rest, if they that kingdom lose.
He who shall do this hath prompt recompense
Henceforth for ever of what may be won
Of gain within these fires.   I let him sit
Beside myself.' . . .

Then God's antagonist arrayed himself
Swift in rich arms.   He had a guileful mind.
The hero set the helmet on his head
And bound it fast, fixed it with clasps.   He knew
Many a speech deceitful; turned him thence,
Hardy of mind, departed through hell's doors,
Striking the flames in two with a fiend's power;
450 Would secretly deceive with wicked deed
Men, the Lord's subjects, that misled, forlorn,
To God they became evil.   So he fared,
Through his fiend's power, till on earth he found
Adam, God's handiwork, with him his wife,
The fairest woman.

HENRY MORLEY.

SELECTIONS FROM THE EXODUS

The *Exodus*, a poem of 589 lines, was one of the series formerly ascribed to Cædmon (see p. 104). Its date and author are unknown; Blackburn, in his edition (Boston, 1907), would place it between *Beowulf* and the Cynewulfian poems (cf. Cook, *Modern Language Notes* **39** 77). The poem gives an account of the departure of the children of Israel from Egypt, beginning with the death of the first-born, and closing with the rejoicing of the Israelites at the destruction of Pharaoh's host.

1. THE PILLAR OF FIRE

Then I have heard that the brave of heart
Blew in the morn a glorious blast
With the blare of trumpets. The troop arose,   100
The force of the brave, the folk of the Lord,
The eager army, as Moses commanded,
The famous captain of kindred hosts.
Ahead they beheld the leader of life [1]
Measure the way of the air ; the cloud
Guided their journey as soon as the seamen [2]
Fared on their way to the sea. The folk
Were joyful, loud was the cry of the host.
 Arose at evening a heavenly beacon,
A second wonder ; after the sunset
They saw the marvel above the people   110

---

[1] The pillar of cloud.   [2] The Israelites.

Shining with flame, a burning pillar.
Above the bowmen the white rays glittered,
The shield-walls shone, the shades departed,
The sloping night-shadows could not cover
Their place of concealment. The candle of heaven
Burned ; a new warden by night was appointed
O'er the army to dwell, lest by fear of the desert,
By sudden seizure, by ocean-like tempests,
The hoary heath should distract their hearts.
120   Had the foregoer locks of fire,
Radiant beams ; with terror of burning,
With heat of flame he threatened the throng
That he should destroy in the desert the host,
Unless they listened, the swift of spirit,
To Moses' voice. The host shone bright,
Glistened the shields ; the warriors saw,
Ready to guide them forth on their way,
The ensign pointing the path direct,
Until, at the edge of the land, the sea
Like a bulwark barred the way of the host.

C. H. A. WAGER.

2. THE MARCHING OF PHARAOH'S HOST

Then the heroes' hearts every one grew hopeless,
For afar they saw, on the southern ways,
The war-array of Pharaoh forward faring.
Sparkled his battle-line, bucklers they were bearing ;
Already whirred the arrows, onward moved the war,
Shields were brightly shining, and the trumpets sang ;
160   There the banners waved, where the war-troop trod.

In circles soared above them the vultures, slaughter-
    seekers,
Hungry for the fighting; [above them flew the raven,]
Dusky carrion-lover, on his dewy wing,
Over those dead warriors.   There the wolves howled
A direful even-song, deeming their food was nigh.

3. THE DESTRUCTION OF THE EGYPTIANS

Then with blood-clots was the blue sky blotted;
Then the resounding ocean, that road of seamen,
Threatened bloody horror, till by Moses' hand
The great lord of fate freed the mad waters.
Wide the sea drove, swept with its death-grip,   480
Foamed all the deluge, the doomed ones yielded,
Seas fell on that track, all the sky was troubled,
Fell those steadfast ramparts, down crashed the floods.
Melted were those sea-towers, when the mighty One,
Lord of heaven's realm, smote with holy hand
Those heroes strong as pines, that people proud. . . .
The yawning sea was mad,
Up it drew, down swirled; dread stood about them,   490
Forth welled the sea-wounds.   On those war-troops fell,
As from the heaven high, that handiwork of God.
Thus swept He down the sea-wall, foamy-billowed,
The sea that never shelters, struck by His ancient sword,
Till, by its dint of death, slept the doughty ones;
An army of sinners, fast surrounded there,
The sea-pale, sodden warriors their souls up yielded.
Then the dark upweltering, of haughty waves the
    greatest,

Over them spread ; all the host sank deep.

500   And thus were drowned the doughtiest of Egypt,
Pharaoh with his folk.   That foe to God,
Full soon he saw, yea, e'en as he sank,
That mightier than he was the Master of the waters,
With His death-grip, determined to end the battle,
Angered and awful.

HENRY S. CANBY.

JUDITH

The *Judith*, whose author is unknown, has been conjecturally
assigned to two different dates, — approximately the years 856 and
915 ; for the respective arguments see Cook's edition and Foster's
Judith: Studies in Metre, Language, and Style.   Authorities agree
that it has Cynewulfian peculiarities, and therefore was probably
written by some admirer of that poet, and that it was certainly
composed before 937, since it is imitated in the *Battle of Brunanburh* (see p. 25), which bears that date.   Its source is found in
various passages of the apocryphal book of Judith, between
7. 33 and 16. 1.   The art and vigor of the poem are equally
remarkable; though apparently only a fragment, one scarcely
misses the part which is lost.   According to Sweet, it combines
the 'highest dramatic and constructive power with the utmost
brilliance of language and metre.'

1. THE FEAST

She doubted not the glorious Maker's gifts
In this wide earth ; from the great Lord to find
Ready protection when she needed most
Grace from the highest Judge ; that He, whose power
Is over all beginnings, with His peace
Would strengthen her against the highest terror.
Therefore the Heavenly Father, bright of mood,
Gave her her wish, because she ever had
Firm faith in the Almighty.

Then heard I Holofernes bade prepare
Wine quickly, with all wonders gloriously
Prepare a feast, to which the chief of men
10 Bade all his foremost thanes, and with great haste
Shield-warriors obeyed, came journeying
To the rich lord, the leader of the people.
That was the fourth day after Judith, shrewd
Of thought, with elfin beauty, sought him first.
Then to the feast they went to sit in pride
At the wine-drinking, all his warriors
Bold in their war-shirts, comrades in his woe.
There were deep bowls oft to the benches borne,
Cups and full jugs to those who sat in hall.
The famed shield-warriors shared the feast, death-doomed,
20 Though that the chief, dread lord of earls, knew not.
Then Holofernes, the gold-friend of man,
Joyed in the pouring out, laughed, talked aloud,
Roared and uproared, that men from far might hear
How the stern-minded stormed and yelled in mirth,
Much bidding the bench-sitters bear their part
Well in the feasting.   So the wicked one
Through the day drenched his followers with wine,
30 The haughty gift-lord, till they lay in swoon ;
His nobles all o'erdrenched as they were struck
To death, and every good poured out of them.

2.   THE SLAYING OF HOLOFERNES

So bade the lord of men serve those in hall
Till the dark night drew near the sons of men.
Then bade the malice-blind to fetch with speed

The blessed maid, ring-wreathed, to his bed-rest.
The attendants quickly did as bade their lord,
Head of mailed warriors, in a twinkling went
To the guest-chamber, where they Judith found   40
Prudent in soul, and then shield-warriors
Began to lead the pious, the bright maid
To the tent, the high one, where within at night
The chief at all times rested, Holofernes,
Hateful to God the Savior.   There was hung
All golden a fair fly-net round the bed
Of the folk-leader, that the baleful one,
The chief of warriors, might look through on each
Child of the brave who came therein, and none   50
Might look on him of mankind, save 't were one
Of his own ill-famed warriors whom the proud one
Bade to draw near, gone in for secret council.
Then they brought quickly to his place of rest
The woman wise of wit ; went rugged men
To make known to their lord that there was brought
The holy woman to his bower tent.
     Then was the famed one blithe of mood, the chief
Of cities thought the bright maid to defile
With filth and stain, but that the glorious Judge
Would not allow, who kept the flock of fame ;
The Lord, who guides the good, stayed him in that.   60
Then went the devilish one, with crowd of men,
Baleful, to seek his bed, where he should lose
His prosperous life, at once, within a night ;
There had he to await his end, on earth
A bitter one, such as he in old time
Wrought for himself, while he, bold chief of men,

Dwelt on this earth under the roof of clouds.
So drunken then with wine the king fell down
In the midst of his bed, that counsel he knew none
Within the chamber of his thought.   Out from within
70   Marched with all haste the warriors steeped in wine,
Who led the faithless, hated chief to bed
For the last time.   The Savior's handmaid then
Gloried, intently mindful how she might
Take from the hateful one most easily
His life before the drunkard woke to shame.

Then she of braided locks, the Maker's maid,
Took a sharp sword, hard from the grinding, drew it
With strong palm from the sheath, and then by name
80   Began to name heaven's Warden, Savior
Of all who dwell on earth, and spake these words :
'God, first Creator, Spirit of comfort, Son
Of the Almighty, glorious Trinity,
I will pray for Thy mercy upon me
Who need it.   Strongly is my heart now stirred,
Distressed the mind sorely disturbed with care ;
Give to me, Lord of heaven, victory
And true belief, that with this sword I may
90   Hew at this giver of death.   Grant me success,
Strong Lord of men ; never had I more need
Of Thy compassion ; now, O mighty Lord,
Bright-minded giver of renown, avenge
What stirs my mood to anger, mind to hate.'
He then, the highest Judge, encouraged her
At once with strength ; so doth He to each one
Of those here dwelling who seek Him for help
With reason and with true belief.   Her mood

Then became unoppressed, and renovate
With holy hope ; she took the heathen then
Fast by his hair, and drew him with her hands
Shamefully towards her, and laid with skill   100
The hateful man where she most easily
Might have the wicked one within her power.
She, braided-locked, then struck the scather-foe
With glittering sword, him in whose thought was hate,
That she cut half his neck through, and he lay
In swoon, drunk, with a death-wound, but not yet
Was dead, his soul all fled ; the woman then,
Famous for strength, with vigor struck again
The heathen dog, so that his head went forth   110
Upon the floor.   Then the foul carcase lay
Empty behind, while the soul went elsewhere
Under the abyss, and there it was condemned,
Tied down to torment ever after, wound
About with serpents, fixed to punishment,
Chained in hell's burning after it went hence.
Nor must he hope at all, in darkness whelmed,
That he can come thence from the serpent's hall,
But there shall dwell ever and ever more
Forth without end in the dark cavern-home,   120
Deprived for ever of the joys of light.

3.   THE RETURN TO BETHULIA

Great glory Judith then had gained in strife,
As God, the Lord of Heaven, granted her,
Who gave her victory.   The clear-witted maid
Then quickly brought the leader's bleeding head

Into the bag that her attendant maid,
A pale-faced woman, trained to noble ways,
Had carried thither with the food of both,
And Judith, thoughtful-minded, gave it then,
130   So gory, to her maid to carry home.
Then both the women went directly thence
Bold in their strength, exulting in success,
Out from that host, till they might clearly see
The glittering walls of fair Bethulia.
They then, adorned with bracelets, sped on foot
140   Forth until, glad of mood, they had gone on
To the wall-gate.   Sat warriors, men on watch,
Kept guard within the fortress, as before
Judith had bidden them in their distress,
The snare-devising maid, famed for her strength,
When she went forth upon her path of war.
Then she was come again, dear to her folk,
And then forthwith the prudent woman bade
Some of the men of the wide burgh go forth
150   To meet her, and to let her quickly in
Through the wall's gate, and to the victor folk
Spake thus : ' I now can tell you of a thing
Worth thanks, that ye no longer need to mourn.
Blithe to you is the Creator, Glory of kings ;
Throughout the wide world that has been made known,
That glorious prosperity now shines
Brightly upon you, glory now is given
For all the evils that ye long have borne.'
160   Then were the burghers blithe when they had heard
Over the high wall how the holy maid
Spake to them.   In the army there was joy ;

The people hastened to the fortress-gate,
Women and men together crush and crowd,
In bands, in bodies, thronged and ran, old, young,
Towards the handmaid of the Lord by thousands.
Within that festive city every man
Was gladdened in his spirit when they knew
That it was Judith come back to her home,
Quickly with reverence they then let her in. 170
 The prudent one, adorned with gold, then bade
Her servant, grateful-minded, to unwrap
The head of the war-chieftain, and to the eyes
Of the burghers show it, bloody, as a sign
How she had sped in the contest. Then to all
The people spake the noble woman : ' Here,
Men famed for victory, the people's leaders,
Here ye may plainly gaze upon the head
Of the most hated heathen warrior,
The lifeless Holofernes, of all men 180
He who for us most shaped sore care and death,
And worse would add, but God denied to him
A longer life to afflict us with his feuds.
Through help of God I forced his life from him.
Now my will is to bid each man of you,
Burghers, shield-warriors, that you instantly
Be ready for the fight. When from the east
God the Creator, holy King, has sent 190
A ray of light, bear forth your shields on breast,
Fire-hardened corslets, and bright helms among
The horde of scathers, with your glittering swords
To slay the death-doomed leaders of the folk,
The fated chiefs. Your foes are doomed to death,

And ye have power and glory in the fight,
As through my hand the mighty Lord hath shown
    you.'

4. THE BATTLE

Then a bold host was suddenly prepared
200 Of men keen for the conflict.   Famed for courage
Soldiers and nobles marched, bore flags, straight forth
Helmeted men went from the holy burgh,
At the first reddening of dawn, to fight ;
Loud stormed the din of shields.
For that rejoiced the lank wolf in the wood,
And the black raven, slaughter-greedy bird ;
Both knew that men of the land thought to achieve
A slaughter of the fated ones.   Then flew
210 The eagle, dewy-feathered, on their track,
Eager for prey ; the sallow-coated bird
Sang with its horny beak the song of war.
Warriors, brave men, marched to the battle,
They who not long before suffered reproach
From the foreigners, shame from the heathen.   But all
That was hard was repaid at the play of the spears
To Assyria, when under their war-flags came
220 The Hebrews to the tents.   Then boldly they
Let fly the showers of arrows, snakes of war,
From the horned bows the arrows firm in place.
Loud stormed the angry warriors, spears were sent
Amidst the throng of bold ones, men were wroth,
Men of the land against the hated race,
Marched stern of mood, rugged of mind, to take
Hard vengeance on old foes weary with mead.

The soldiers drew with hands their clear-marked swords, 230
Proved edges, slew the Assyrian warriors
Attempting evil, slew with zeal, spared none
Of all the army, whether wretch or rich,
Of living men whom they could overtake.

5. THE SEEKING OF HOLOFERNES

So all the morning-time the kinsman-troops
Pursued the stranger on their native soil,
Till the chief watchmen of the host, in wrath,
Saw that the Hebrews strongly showed to them   240
The swing of swords.   They went to make that known
In words to the chief thanes.   They roused the highest,
And fearfully told him, mead-weary man,
The dreadful tale, the morning's quick alarm,
The cruel edge-play.   Suddenly, I heard,
The hero doomed to slaughter leapt from sleep,
And hosts of men sought the pavilion
Of baleful Holofernes, thronged in crowds ;
They only thought to offer him their help,   250
Their lord, before the terror came on him,
The power of the Hebrews.   All supposed
The lord of men and the bright maid together
Were in the shining tent, the noble Judith
And he, the lustful, loathsome, terrible.
None was there of the earls who dared to wake,
Or learn how it had been to the great chief
With the holy woman the handmaid of God.   260
Nearer the people of the Hebrews drew,
Fought stiffly with war-weapons, hilts, bright swords,

Requited old assaults, all grievances.
In that day's work Assyria was subdued,
Its pride was bowed.   Men stood about the tent
Of the chief, much stirred, and gloom was in their minds.
Then all together they cried noisily,
270 Began to clamor loudly, gnash their teeth,
Void of all good, setting their teeth in wrath ;
Then was their glory, ease, power, at its end.
The earls thought so to waken their dear Lord,
But not a whit succeeded.   Then was found
One of the warriors so resolute
That, hard in hate, within the bower-tent
He ventured, as need urged him ; on the bed
Found his gold-giver lying pale, soul gone,
280 Deprived of life.   Forthwith he, shuddering,
Fell to the ground, in fierce mood, tore his hair
And his robe too, and to the warriors
Who were outside there, joyless, thus he spake :
' Here we may plainly see our fate foreshown,
Sign given us the time presses near with ills,
When we shall perish all, destroyed in battle ;
Here our support, hewn with the sword, lies headless.'
290 They then in bitter mood threw down their arms,
Turned themselves, faint of heart, to haste away
In flight.

6. THE PURSUIT

Upon their track the folk enlarged in might
Fought till the most part of the army lay
In battle sacrificed, upon the field
Of victory, sword-hewn to please the wolves

And to content the birds that crave for slaughter.
They who yet lived fled from the foemen's arms,
The band of Hebrews followed on their track,
Honored with victory, enriched with fame.
The Lord God, the Almighty, graciously 300
Gave them His help. They labored piously,
The famous heroes, with bright swords to cut
A war-path through the press of evil ones,
Hewed shields, cut the defense through ; grim in fight
The Hebrew men were shooting, with desire
Strong in the thanes towards the strife of spears.
　Here fell in dust the greatest part of all
The number of the nobles of Assyria, 310
Race of the enemy ; few came alive
To their own country. Warriors renowned,
Within the place of slaughter, as they fled,
Turned them to reeking corpses. Room was there
For dwellers on the land to take red spoil
From their most hated foes, now dead — shields fair
Adorned, broad swords, brown helms, and costly cups.
The country's guardians, on the people's land,
Had gloriously overcome the foe, 320
And silenced old oppressions with their swords ;
They rested on the path who, when alive,
Of living men were their worst enemies.

7. THE SPOIL

Then for a month's space all men of the tribe,
Greatest of peoples, proud, with plaited locks,
Bore, drew to the bright town, Bethulia,

Helms, hip-knives, corslets, the war-dress of men
330 Gold-fretted, treasure more than cunning man
Can tell.   All this the people of the land
Won with their strength in fight, bold under banners,
Through Judith's prudent teaching, noble maid.
They, the brave earls, brought from the raid for her,
As her own meed, the sword and bloody helm
Of Holofernes, his breast-armor broad
And ornamented with red gold ; and all
340 Of treasure that the haughty chief possessed.
His heritage of circlets and bright gems,
They gave to the bright woman prompt of thought.

8. THE PRAISE

For all this Judith gave to God the praise,
The glorious Lord of men, who gave her honor,
Glory in earth's kingdom and reward in heaven,
In the bright skies reward of victory ;
Because she had a true belief in God
Almighty, and at the end had not a doubt
Of the reward for which she long had yearned.
    For this to latest ages evermore
Be glory unto the dear Lord who made
The wind and air, the heavens and wide earth,
And also the wild streams He made, and He
350 Through His own mercy made the joys of heaven.

HENRY MORLEY.

V

SAINTS' LEGENDS

SELECTIONS FROM THE ANDREAS

The *Andreas*, a poem of 1722 lines, has been called the Christian *Beowulf*, and was certainly written with *Beowulf* as a model. It is now generally agreed that Cynewulf was not responsible for it. A possible author might have been Bishop Acca of Hexham (ca. 660–740), a devoted disciple and companion of Bishop Wilfrith, himself from his earliest manhood (653) a votary of St. Andrew, whose equal he was in some quarters eventually accounted to be. When Wilfrith died in 709, Acca succeeded him as Bishop of Hexham until 731, and there completed the great church which Wilfrith had erected in honor of the saint. Here he gathered legends and relics of saints; gave much attention to music, in which he was a proficient; induced Bede to write a Latin poem, eventually translated into Old English; and (before 716) exhorted that scholar (d. 735) to transmit his name to posterity, by means which he indicated. His dates would admit of the *Andreas* falling in time between *Beowulf* (above, p. 9) and the Cynewulfian poems (p. 79). For details, see Cook, *Trans. Conn. Acad. of Arts and Sciences* 25 249–329.

The standard edition is by Krapp (Boston, 1906).

The poem narrates the adventures of St. Andrew, who crosses the sea to the Mermedonians, a race of cannibals, in order to rescue St. Matthew, whom they are holding captive. Christ, in the guise of a young shipmaster, carries him to his destination. Matthew is set free; Andrew performs a miracle, and converts the people.

133

1. ST. ANDREW GOES DOWN TO THE SEA

So at the dawning, when the day first broke,
He gat him o'er the sand-downs to the sea,
Valiant in heart, and with him went his thanes
To walk upon the shingle, where the waves
Loud thundered, and the streams of ocean beat
Against the shore.   Full glad was that brave saint
240 To see upon the sands a galley fair
Wide-bosomed.   Then, behold, resplendent dawn,
Brightest of beacons, came upon her way,
Hasting from out the murky gloom of night,
And heaven's candle shone across the floods.
Three seamen saw he there, a glorious band,
Courageous men, upon their ocean-bark
Sitting all ready to depart, like men
Just come across the deep.   The Lord Himself
It was, the everlasting Lord of hosts,
Almighty, with His holy angels twain.
250 In raiment they were like seafaring men,
These heroes, like to wanderers on the waves,
When in the flood's embrace they sail with ships
Upon the waters cold to distant lands.

2. A STORM AT SEA

Then was the ocean stirred
370 And deeply troubled, then the horn-fish played,
Shot through the raging deep ; the sea-gull gray,
Greedy for slaughter, flew in circling flight.
The candle of the sky grew straightway dark,

The winds waxed strong, the waves whirled, and the surge
Leapt high, the ropes creaked, dripping with the waves ;
The Terror of the waters rose, and stood
Above them with the might of multitudes.
The thanes were sore afraid ; not one of them
Dared hope that he would ever reach the land,
Of those who by the sea had sought a ship
With Andrew, for as yet they did not know   380
Who pointed out the course for that sea-bark.

3. ANDREW TELLS HOW CHRIST STILLED THE
TEMPEST

                              I know
Myself that there is One who shieldeth us,
The Maker of the angels, Lord of hosts.
Rebuked and bridled by the King of might,
The Terror of the waters shall grow calm,
The leaping sea.   So once in days of yore
Within a bark upon the struggling waves
We tried the waters, riding on the surge,
And very fearful seemed the sad sea-roads.   440
The ocean-floods beat fierce against the shores ;
Oft wave would answer wave ; and whiles upstood
From out the ocean's bosom, o'er our ship,
A Terror on the breast of our sea-boat.
There on that ocean-courser bode His time
The glorious God, Creator of mankind,
Almighty One.   The men were filled with fear,
They sought protection, mercy from the Lord.
And when that company began to call,

450 The King straightway arose, and stilled the waves,
The seething of the waters — He who gives
Bliss to the angels; He rebuked the winds;
The sea subsided, and the boundaries
Of ocean-stream grew calm.   Then laughed our soul,
When under heaven's course our eyes beheld
The winds and waves and Terror of the deep
Affrighted by the Terror of the Lord.

4. THE VISION OF ANDREW'S DISCIPLES

His noble followers answered him again,
Giving reply from out their inmost souls: —
'Our journey, Andrew, will we tell to thee,
860 That wisely thou mayst understand in heart: —
A sleep came o'er us weary of the sea,
And eagles came across the struggling waves
In flight, exulting in their mighty wings,
And while we slept they took our souls away;
With joy they bore us flying through the air,
Gracious and bright, rejoicing in their speed;
And gently they caressed us, while they hymned
Continual praise; there was unceasing song
870 Throughout the sky; a beauteous host was there,
A glorious multitude.   The angels stood
About the Prince, the thanes about their Lord,
In thousands; in the highest they gave praise
With holy voice unto the Lord of lords;
The angel-band rejoiced.   We there beheld
The holy patriarchs and a mighty troop
Of martyrs; to the Lord victorious

That righteous throng sang never-ending praise;
And David too was with them, Jesse's son,
The King of Israel, blessed warrior,   880
Come to Christ's throne.   Likewise we saw you twelve
All standing there before the Son of God,
Full glorious men of great nobility;
Archangels holy throned in majesty
Did serve you; happy is it for the man
Who may enjoy that bliss.   High joy was there,
Glory of warriors, an exalted life;
Nor was there sorrow there for any man.
Drear exile, open torment, is the lot
Of him who must be stranger to those joys,
And wander wretched when he goes from hence.'   890

5. ST. ANDREW'S MIRACLE

Then was there no delay; straightway the stone
Split open, and a stream came rushing out
And flowed along the ground; at early dawn
The foaming billows covered up the earth;
The ocean-flood waxed great; mead was outpoured
After that day of feasting!   Mail-clad men
Shook off their slumbers; water deeply stirred
Seized on the earth; the host was sore dismayed
At terror of the flood; the youths were doomed,   1530
And perished in the deep; the rush of war
Snatched them away with tumult of the sea.
That was a grievous trouble, bitter beer;
The ready cup-bearers did not delay;
From daybreak on each man had drink to spare.

The might of waters waxed, the men wailed loud,
Old bearers of the spear ; they strove to flee
The fallow stream ; they fain would save their lives
And seek a refuge in the mountain caves,
1540 Firm earth's support.   An angel drove them back,
Compassing all the town with gleaming fire,
With savage flames.   Wild beat the sea within ;
No troop of men could scape from out the walls.
The waves waxed, and the waters thundered loud ;
The firebrands flew ; the flood welled up in streams.

ROBERT K. ROOT.

SELECTIONS FROM THE ELENE

The *Elene* is certainly by Cynewulf, since it contains his name
in runes (see p. 141). For a discussion of its date, see p. 79.
The source of the poem is a legend of the Invention of the Cross
similar to, but not identical with, that contained in the *Acta
Sanctorum* for May 4.

The poem tells how Constantine, on the eve of a battle with
the Huns, has a vision of the cross. Constantine, being victorious
in the battle, sends his mother, Helena, to the Holy Land, to seek
the true original of the sacred emblem. She finds three crosses, and,
by means of a miracle, is enabled to determine the one on which
Christ was crucified.

The most recent edition is that of Cook, *The Old English Elene,
Phœnix, and Physiologus* (New Haven and London, 1919). There
are translations by Weymouth (1888), Garnett (1889), and Kennedy
(*The Poems of Cynewulf*).

1. THE BATTLE

Trumpets resounded before the troop.   110
The raven was watching and waiting joyfully,
The dewy-winged eagle saw from the distance,
And the wolf from his haunt in the desolate wood
Howled at the terror of death and hate.
Arrows rained on them as they rushed together;
Shields were broken, javelins shattered,
And the sword that swayed with the swinging arm
Came crashing down on the death-doomed foe.
They pressed on resolutely, pushing with effort,
Thrusting with swords and swinging battle-axes,

And ever their banner was borne forward
With shouts of triumph that were loud and shrill,
As the heathen fell joyless on that field.
Hastily the host of Huns fled away
When the Roman king, the fighter unconquerable,
The fierce leader, lifted the cross.
Wide was the ruin that was wrought on the heathen.
Some perished there in that place of death,
Some fled half alive to rocky fastnesses,
And won their way back to Danube's banks;
And some found death in the depths of the lake-stream
But the proud victors chased the vanquished
From the day's dawning till night came down,
And with ash-darts and arrows (fierce battle-adders)
They destroyed the hateful host of the enemy.

CHARLTON M. LEWIS.

2. THE VOYAGE

Over the billows where rolled the monsters of the deep
they let the towering sea-racers rush on in foam; often
did the ship's side receive above the watery tumult the
240 buffets of the waves; the music of ocean resounded.
Never before nor since have I heard that a woman con-
ducted a fairer force over the ocean-stream, the highway
of the sea. There he who beheld their course could see
the timbered ship bound over the bath-way, fleet under
the swelling sails, could see the ocean-courser play, the
wave-floater glide. Joyful were the spirited warriors,
and the queen delighted in the voyage, when once the
ring-prowed vessels had traversed the stronghold of the

main, and arrived at their haven in the land of the Greeks. 250
They let their barks, the old sea-dwellings, await at the
shore, fast at their anchors, buffeted with sand, the
council of heroes, what time the warlike queen should
again repair to them over the eastern ways with a multitude of men.

3. AUTOBIOGRAPHIC RUNE-PASSAGE

This passage is of much importance for the biography of
Cynewulf, but it is difficult, and in some places obscure. The
words in small capitals represent the runes of the original. See
Cook's *The Christ of Cynewulf*, pp. lxvi ff., 151 ff. A similar
rune-passage from the *Christ* will be found above (p. 83).

Thus I, old and ready to depart by reason of the
treacherous house, have woven wordcraft and wondrously
gathered, have now and again pondered and sifted my
thought in the prison of the night.   I knew not all concerning the right . . . [1] before wisdom, through the noble 1240
power, revealed a larger view into the cogitation of my
heart.   I was guilty of misdeeds, fettered by sins, tor-
mented with anxieties, bound with bitternesses, beset
with tribulations, before he bestowed inspiration through
the bright order [2] as a help to the aged man.   The
mighty King granted me His blameless grace and shed
it into my mind, revealed it as glorious, and in course
of time dilated it ; He set my body free, unlocked my 1250
heart, and released the power of song, which I have
since joyfully made use of in the world.   Not once

[1] Perhaps something lost.
[2] *Or*, gloriously.

alone, but many times, I reflected on the tree of glory,
before I had the miracle disclosed concerning the glorious
tree, as in the course of events I found related in books,
in writings, concerning the sign of victory.   Until that
the man [1] had always been buffeted by billows of sorrow,
was an expiring TORCH, though he in the mead-hall had
1260 received treasures, appled gold.   Y (?) lamented; the
FORCED companion suffered affliction, an oppressive
secret, though [2] before him the STEED measured the
mile-paths and proudly ran, decked with wires.[3]   Joy
has waned, pleasure has decreased with the years; youth
has fled, the former pride.   U (?) was of old the splendor
of youth; now, after the allotted time, are the days
departed, the joys of life have vanished, as WATER glides
1270 away, the hurrying floods.   Every one's WEALTH is tran-
sitory under the sky; the ornaments of the field pass
away under the clouds like the wind when it rises loud
before men, roams among the clouds, rushes along in
rage, and again on a sudden grows still, close locked
within its prison, held down by force.

ALBERT S. COOK.

[1] Emending *sæc* to *secg*.
[2] Emending *þær* to *þeah*.
[3] i.e. metal ornaments.

VI

RELIGIOUS MYTHOLOGY

THE PHŒNIX

Author and date are unknown, but the poem may not improbably have been written by Cynewulf; cf. Cook, *The Old English Elene, Phœnix, and Physiologus*, pp. xxvi–xxviii.

The poem is based upon the *Carmen de Phœnice* of Lactantius, the 'Christian Cicero,' who flourished about 300 A.D., a work which is conceived in the Christian spirit (cf. Cook's edition, pp. xxxvi–xxxviii). This Latin poem consists of only 170 lines, as against the 677 of the Old English, and corresponds to vv. 1–380 of the latter. The rest of the Old English poem seems to be original, with the exception of certain hints derived from Philip the Presbyter's († 456) commentary on Job. The first eight lines of the Latin, which follow, correspond to the first thirty-two lines of the Old English :

> Est locus in primo felix oriente remotus
> Qua patet æterni maxima porta poli,
> Nec tamen æstivos hiemisve propinquus ad ortus,
> Sed qua sol verno fundit ab axe diem.
> Illic planities tractus diffundit apertos,
> Nec tumulus crescit, nec cava vallis hiat ;
> Sed nostros montes, quorum juga celsa putantur,
> Per bis sex ulnas eminet ille locus.

Among the Biblical passages which may be referred to in the original Latin poem are the following : Gen. 2. 8, 10 ; 7. 19, 20 ; Ezek. 47. 7–12 ; John 4. 10, 14 ; Rom. 6. 5, 8–10 (cf. *Ph.* 368–370);

Rev. 20. 2–7 ; 22. 1, 2.   The converse of Virg. *Æn.* 6. 273 ff. has
been found in our poem, vv. 50 ff. ; the reflection of a verse of
Ennius, ' Mi soli cæli maxima porta patet,' in vv. 11, 12 (cf. Lact.
Inst. 1. 18. 11) ; Ovid, *Am.* 2. 6. 54 in v. 87 ; *Met.* 15. 392 ff. in
various parts.

Correspondences within the poem are such as 1 ff. with 393 ff.,
611 ff. ; 50 ff. with 611 ff. ; 153 ff. with 411 ff., 426 ff., 437 ff. ;
163 ff., 337 ff., with 539 ff., 590 ff. ; 188 ff. with 451 ff., 526 ff.,
650 ff. ; 222 ff. with 646 ff. ; 265 ff. with 575 ff.

The descriptions are noticeable, particularly those of the Phœnix,
of the Paradisal grove, of the sunrise, and of music.

1. THE PARADISE OF THE PHŒNIX

Far away to the East there lies, so I have heard, the
noblest of lands, famous among men.   This region is
not accessible to many rulers in the world, but is removed
by the power of God from the workers of evil.   Beauteous **is** that plain, gladdened with joys, with the sweetest
odors of earth.   Peerless is the island, noble the Creator,
10 high-hearted and abounding in power, who established
that land.   Before the blessed ones heaven's door
often stands open, and the transport of its melodies is
revealed.   Winsome is that champaign, with green
forests stretching wide beneath the skies.   There neither
rain, nor snow, nor breath of frost, nor blaze of fire, nor
downpour of hail, nor fall of hoar-frost, nor heat of sun,
nor ever-during cold, nor warm weather, nor winter
shower, works aught of harm ; but unscathed and
20 flourishing the plain ever abides.   That noble land is
blowing with blossoms.   There neither hills nor mountains stand steep, nor do crags tower high, as here with
us ; there slope no glens nor dales, no mountain-caves,

nor mounds, nor banks, nor aught that is rugged; but
the noble field flourishes beneath the clouds, burgeon-
ing with delights.

That glorious land, as sages reveal to us in their
writings, is twelve cubits higher than any mountain 30
which here with us towers brightly beneath the stars of
heaven.   Serene is that field of victory; there gleams
the sunny grove, the fair forest; the bright fruitage
falls not, but the trees stand ever green, as God commanded them.   Winter and summer alike the forest is
hung with fruits.   The leaves wither not beneath the
sky, nor will fire ever injure them until the final change 40
shall pass upon the world.   As, long ago, when the
onset of waters, the flood of ocean, covered the whole
world, the face of the earth, this noble plain stood
scathless and shielded against the rush of angry billows,
happy and inviolate through the grace of God, so shall
it abide blooming until the Lord's judgment shall come
with flame, what time the halls of death, the dark abodes
of men, shall open to the day.

In that land there is no enemy, neither weeping nor 50
misery, no sign of woe, nor age, nor sorrow, nor pinch-
ing death, nor loss of life, nor coming of harm, neither
sin, nor strife, nor tribulation, nor struggle of poverty,
nor lack of wealth, nor anxiety, nor sleep, nor sore
disease.   Neither do winter's missiles, nor fierce change
of weather beneath the sky, nor the hard frost with its
chill icicles, smite any one.

There neither hail nor hoar-frost nor windy cloud 60
descends to the earth, nor does water fall smitten by the
wind, but wondrous streams spring up as wells, and the

winsome waters from the middle of the wood irrigate the soil with their fair flowing. Every month they burst sea-cold from the greensward, and in their seasons traverse gloriously the grove; for so is the Lord's behest that twelve times the best of floods shall gush
70 through that noble land.

The groves are hung with lovely fruits; the holy ornaments of the wood never wane beneath the heavens, nor do the blossoms, the beauty of the trees, fall to earth; but there on the trees the laden branches, with fruit ever-new, stand splendidly on that meadow, for ever green. Gayly decked by the might of the holy One,
80 that bright forest knows no interruption of its beauty, and holy fragrance floats throughout that blissful land. Never shall aught of change befall it until He who in the beginning established the masterly creation shall bring it to an end.

2. THE ATTENDANT OF THE SUN

A bird wondrously beautiful, strong of pinion, called Phœnix, inhabits this forest; there the dauntless solitary keeps his dwelling and passes his life. Never shall death injure him in that delightful plain while the world endures.
90 Men say that there he observes the course of the sun, ready to meet the candle of God, the flashing jewel; eagerly he watches for the time when that noblest star, the Father's primal work, the refulgent sign of God, shall rise radiant from the east over the billowy ocean, glowing in its splendor. The stars are

hid, gone beneath the western waves or lost in the
dawn, and black night is passing away ; then the bird,
proud of pinion, strong in flight, gazes intently upon the 100
stream of ocean, over the flood beneath the sky, looking eagerly for the light of heaven to rise over the
broad sea, gliding from the east. Thus the noble bird,
changeless in his beauty, dwells near the fountain beside
the welling streams ; there, before heaven's candle
appears, the glorious one bathes twelve times in the
outflow, and at each bath tastes the sea-cold water from
those delicious well-springs. Then, after his watery 110
play, the mettlesome bird flies aloft to a tree so high
that thence he can most easily observe the advance over
the eastern ways, what time heaven's taper, the efful-
gence of light, shall shine clear over the turmoil of
the sea. The land is embellished, the world is beautified,
as soon as the jewel of glory, the noblest of stars,
illumines the earth from beyond the expanse of ocean.

The moment that the sun mounts high over the salt 120
streams, the gray bird courses radiant from that forest-
tree ; swift of wing he flies through the air, singing and
making melody toward the sun. Then is the bird's
behavior winning ; with spirit elate, exultant in his joy,
he varies his song of clear note more wonderfully than
any son of man ever heard beneath the sky since the
supreme King, Maker of glory, established the world, 130
the heaven and the earth. The notes of his lay are
sweeter and lovelier than musical art can render, more
tunable than aught we know of song. Never was trump,
nor horn, nor thrill of harp, nor any voice of man on
earth, nor organ, nor strain of melody, nor wing of

swan,[1] nor any of the harmonies which God hath created for the cheer of men in this sad world, like unto that

140 descant.[2]   Thus he warbles and carols, transported with delight, until the sun descends in the southern sky ; then, silent and attentive, but bold and sagacious, he lifts his head, thrice claps his swift pinions, and then is still. So ever, twelve times by day and by night, he marks the hours.

3. THE FLIGHT AND THE NEW BIRTH

Thus it is appointed to the inhabitant of the wood that he may enjoy the plain to the full, reveling in pro-

150 fusion — in life, and joy, and the adornments of earth, until the keeper of the grove attains a thousand years of this life.   Then the gray-plumed one, ancient and stricken in years, grows burdened.   The choicest of birds flies from the green and blossoming region, and visits a spacious realm of the world, where none abide, as his dwelling-place and home.   There, eminent in power, he gains lordship over the nation of birds,

160 advanced among them, and for a season dwells in the wilderness.   Then, strong in flight, though weighed down with years, he departs westward, flying on swift pinions.   All about their noble leader throng the birds, every one desiring to be minister and attendant to the illustrious chief, until he gains the land of the Syrians with a countless retinue.   Here the pure one thrusts them abruptly away, so that he tenants a desolate and

---

[1] Cf. *The Swan*, p. 72.
[2] Cf. Tennyson, *The Holy Grail* 113–5.

shadowy spot in a grove, sequestered and hidden from 170
the throng of men.   There he occupies in the forest a
lofty tree, firmly rooted beneath the cope of heaven,
a tree which men on earth call Phœnix, from the name
of the bird.   The illustrious King, Lord of mankind,
hath granted to this tree, so I have heard, that of all
trees growing high over the earth it shall blossom bright
beyond the rest ; nothing mischievous can wickedly harm
it, but it remains ever defended and scathless while the 180
world endures.

When the wind is at rest, the weather is fair, the holy
jewel of heaven shines clear, the clouds are dispersed,
the raging waters stand still, every storm beneath the
sky is calmed, and warm from the south shines the
candle of the sky, giving light to multitudes, then he
begins to build upon the boughs and make ready his
nest.   Great is then his longing swiftly to convert, by 190
the activity of his mind, old age to life, and thus renew
his youth.   From far and near he gathers the sweetest
and most delightful plants and the leafage of the forest,
assembling them at his dwelling-place ; nay, more, the
perfume of every delightsome plant which the King of
glory, the Father of all beginnings, fashioned throughout
the earth as a blessing to mankind, even the sweetest
odors beneath the sky.   These bright treasures he conveys by himself to the interior of the tree, and there in 200
the wilderness the wild bird builds his beauteous and
winsome house on its lofty top.   There he dwells in his
upper chamber, encompassing in the leafy shade his
body and plumage with holy spices and the noblest
shoots of the earth.

While the sun, the jewel of heaven, shines hottest
above the shadow in the summer time, he sits, ready for
210 departure, surveying the world and enduring his fate.
Suddenly his house becomes ignited by reason of the
radiant sun ; the spices glow, and the pleasant hall fumes
with the sweet odors ; the bird and his nest burn together
in that fierce heat, laid hold of by the fire.   The pyre is
kindled ; fire enfolds the disconsolate creature's house ;
fiercely devouring, the yellow flame hastens ; the Phœnix, old with long-past years, is consumed, when once
the fire has seized upon his perishing body ; his life, the
220 doomed one's soul, escapes, when the flame of the funeral
pile consumes flesh and bone.

Yet in due season new life returns to him, when
once the ashes begin, after the fire's violence, to knit
together, cohering to a ball.   When that bright nest,
the brave bird's abode, is clean demolished by the blaze,
the corpse grows cold, the body is in pieces, and the
230 flames subside.   Then from the ashes of the pyre the likeness of an apple is afterwards found ; out of this grows
a wondrously beautiful worm, as if it had been hatched
from an egg, bright from the shell.   It grows in the
shade, becoming first like the young of an eagle, a fair
nestling ; then thrives joyfully until it resembles in
size an old eagle ; and afterward is decked with plumage,
240 brightly blooming as at the first.   His flesh is then all
renewed, born again, sundered from sin.   It is as
when one brings home for food at harvest, at reaping-
time, the fruits of the earth, pleasant nourishment,
before the coming on of winter, lest the rain-storm
should spoil them beneath the skies ; and so men find

support, the delights of sustenance, when frost and snow shall with excessive might deck the earth in the garments of winter. From these fruits shall the riches 250 of men again arise, by reason of the nature of grain, which is sown at the first as a pure seed, but when in spring the sun's rays, the sign of life, waken the wealth of the world, the fruits, the garniture of earth, are again brought forth by their own nature. So in like manner the bird, old in years, grows once more young, wrought round with flesh. He toucheth no earthly food, save that he tastes of the honey-dew which 260 oft descends at midnight ; with this the noble bird supports his life until he again visits his own dwelling-place, his ancient home.

4. THE RETURN

When the bird, proud of pinion, hath arisen from the midst of the spicery, his life renewed, young and full of endowments, he collects from the dust the active body which fire had snatched away, the leavings of flame ; after the rush of flame he deftly gathers the ruinous 270 bones, assembling both bones and embers, the relics of the pyre, and covers the booty of death with herbage, splendidly adorning it. He is now eager to revisit his own haunts, so he grasps with his feet, seizes with his talons, the leavings of flame, and joyously directs his flight toward his home, his sun-bright seat, his blessed fatherland. He is wholly restored in life and plumage as he was in the beginning, when victorious God first 280 set him in that noble plain. There with the ashes he

brings his own bones, which the fury of fire had wrapped in flame on the mound ; these the warlike one buries in that isle, bones and embers together.   Renewed in himself is the ministrant of the sun, what time the luminary of heaven, the most flashing of jewels, the chief of
290 noble stars, rises over ocean in splendor from the east.

5. THE ASPECT OF THE PHŒNIX

In front the bird is gay of hue, with play of bright colors about the breast; the back of his head is green, curiously shot with crimson ; his tail is splendidly diversified, now dusky, now crimson, now cunningly splotched with silver.   The tips of the wings are white, the neck green below and above ; the beak shines like glass or
300 gems, so lustrous are the jaws within and without. His eye is piercing, and likest in color to a gleaming precious stone, set in gold by the art of the goldsmith. About his neck is the brightest of collars, woven of feathers, like the orb of the sun.   Marvelous is his body beneath, wondrous beautiful, comely and resplendent ; the shield over the bird's back is exquisitely fitted
310 together ; his legs and tawny feet are overgrown with scales.   In appearance the bird is every way most like, as books relate, to a peacock, happy in its rearing.   Not dull is he nor sluggish, not heavy nor torpid, like some birds that slowly wing their flight through the air ; but he is nimble and swift and full light, beauteous and charming, and gloriously marked.   Eternal is the Sovran who grants him blessedness.

6. THE RETINUE OF BIRDS

Then he departs from this country to visit the fields, 320
his ancient dwelling-place.   The bird flies, manifest to
the peoples, to many men throughout the world; they
assemble in troops from south and from north, from east
and from west; they journey in hosts from far and near to
the spot where they behold in the bird the fair display of
the Creator's grace, even as the King of victory assigned
him in the beginning a peculiar nature, attractions above 330
the race of birds.   Then men upon earth wonder at his
comeliness and form; books tell, and they designate with
their hands in marble, when the day and the hour are to
manifest to the multitudes the perfections of the swift flyer.

Then the nation of birds press in on every side in
throngs, coming from distant ways.   They praise and
celebrate in song, in words of power, that noble one;
they surround the holy creature with a ring in that
flight through the air; in the midst is the Phœnix, 340
encircled by multitudes.   The people gaze, wondering
how the devoted retinue honors the bird, one band after
another making loud proclamation and extolling as their
king the beloved leader of their people.   They joyfully
lead the noble prince to his land, until the solitary one
outstrips them by the speed of his pinions, so that the
flock of rejoicing ones can no longer follow him, when
the delight of the flying hosts is winging his way from
these regions to his native country.

Thus the blessed one revisits his former home, the 350
lovely land, after the hour of his death.   The birds leave
their valiant chief and return sorrowful to their own

country, when the prince is young at home.   God alone
knows, the King almighty, what his sex is, whether
male or female ; no man knows, but only the Creator,
what are the wonderful contrivances, the ancient decree,
360 concerning the bird's nature.

7. DEATH NOT DREADED

There the happy one may enjoy his home and the
fountain-streams in the forests, dwelling on the plain
until a thousand years are past ; then life ends, and the
pyre covers him with kindled flame ; yet once more he
returns to life, strangely awakened.   Therefore, even
when nearing his end, he dreads not the dire agony of
370 death, since he is ever assured of new life after the fury
of flame, of revival after dissolution, being speedily
restored from his ashes in the form of nestling, and
growing young again under the canopy of heaven.

He is his own son, his kindly father, and again the
heir to his ancient inheritance.   The mighty Lord of
mankind granted him to undergo a wondrous change
into that which he had been erewhile, to be encompassed
380 with feathers, though fire snatch him away.

In like manner every blessed soul will choose for himself to enter into everlasting life through death's dark
portal when the present misery is overpast, so that after
his days on earth he may in ever-during jubilee enjoy
the gifts of his Lord, dwelling eternally in that world
as the recompense of his deeds.   Much of a similar sort
does this bird's nature shadow forth concerning Christ's
chosen followers — how in this perilous time they may

possess pure happiness beneath the heavens through the 390
Father's aid, and secure exalted bliss in the home on
high.

8. THE LOSS OF EDEN

We have learned that the Almighty created man and
woman by the plenitude of his marvelous power, and
placed them in the fairest spot of earth, which the children of men call Paradise, where was no lack of bliss so
long as they would keep the word of the Eternal, heark-
ening to the commandment of the Holy One in that
new-created joy.   There malice, the envy of the ancient 400
foe, plagued them ; he offered them as food the fruit of
the tree, so that they both unwarily took of the apple
against the will of God, and tasted of that which was
forbidden.   Then was bitter woe theirs after that repast,
and likewise was it a grievous banquet to their posterity,
their sons and daughters ; . . .[1] they bore God's wrath,
bitter anguish ; their offspring were yet to requite it with
sorrow that they took of that fare against the word of
the Eternal.   Hence it came that they must relinquish 410
in grief the joy of their home by reason of the serpent's
malice ; he, in those far-off days, grievously beguiled our
first parents with his crafty mind, so that they sought
out a life far from thence in this vale of death, a sorrowful abode.   The better life was hidden from them in
seclusion, and the holy plain fast locked against them
for many winters, until the King of glory, the Joy of 420
mankind, the Comfort of the dejected, the only Hope,
once more opened it to the saints.

[1] A line and a half unintelligible.

9. THE SIGNIFICANCE OF THE NEST

Most like is the journey of this bird, as wise men discourse in words and reveal in books. When, grown old, worn down with years, he forsakes his home and fatherland, weary in soul he departs until he finds the lofty
430 shelter of the forest, in which he constructs a new habitation with the noblest twigs and plants, a nest in the grove; he longs, once more grown youthful, to regain, by the blaze of fire, life after death, to become rejuvenated, and, after his bath of flame, to visit again his ancient abode, his sun-bright dwelling.

So our forefathers, our first parents, forsook the beau-
440 teous plain, the lovely seat of glory, and made a long journey into the hand of fiends, where the haters, the wretched monsters, ofttimes molested them. Yet there were many who with holy practices, with glorious deeds, obeyed God, so that the Lord, the Emperor of heaven, was gracious in spirit unto them. That is now the high tree in which the righteous dwell, where none of the ancient foes can in any wise injure them with venom,
450 with any sign of evil, in the perilous time.

The soldier of the Lord makes himself a nest against every attack when he distributes alms to the poor and needy; when he calls to his aid the Lord, the Father; when he hastens forward, extinguishing the transgressions of this fleeting life, and blotting out dark deeds of evil. He keeps the law of God steadfastly in mind; he follows after prayer with pure meditations, and devoutly bows
460 his knee to earth; he flees all evil, ravening sin, in the fear of God; he longs with glad heart to accomplish

every good deed he may ; at all times his shield is God, the King of victory, the Lord of hosts. These are the plants, these the fruit-branches, which the wild bird gathers from far and near beneath the sky unto his dwelling, where he builds a nest wondrously proof against every attack. In this manner do the soldiers of God now perform His will in their abodes with mind 470 and main, striving after glory ; for this the Eternal, the Almighty, will recompense them with a blessed guerdon. From those plants there shall be established for them a mansion in the city of glory, as the recompense of their deeds — because they kept the sacred lore fervently in their souls, and day and night love the Lord with hearts aglow ; with fair faith choose the Beloved above all worldly possessions ; not for them is there hope of joy 480 in clinging to this transient life. Thus the righteous man wins through lifelong effort unending joy, a home in heaven with the King of kings. Then death, the murderous warrior, embattled in arms, snatches away the life of every one, and straightway dispatches the perishing bodies, bereft of their souls, into the lap of earth, where long they shall rest, wrapped in the mold, until the coming of fire.   490

10. THE LAST JUDGMENT [1]

Then shall many of human kind be led into the assembly ; there the Father of angels, the righteous King of victory, the Lord of hosts, will hold a council, and judge with equity. Then shall all men on earth be

[1] Cf. pp. 85 ff., 136.

raised again, as the mighty King, the Prince of angels, the Savior of souls, shall proclaim by sound of trumpet over the wide world; for the righteous black death shall 500 be done away with, by the power of the Lord; the just shall be active, congregating in crowds, when this sinful world shall burn in shame, kindled with fire. Every one shall be dismayed in soul when the fire rends asunder the perishable riches of the world, when the flame lays hold of all the treasures of earth, rapaciously seizing the appled gold, and greedily swallowing the beauties of the field. At that all-revealing time, the fair 510 and agreeable interpretation of this bird shall become clear to men, when the King shall raise up all that are in the graves, gathering the bones, assembling limbs and body with the spirit of life before the knee of Christ. From His throne the King, the beauteous Jewel of glory, shall shine in His majesty upon His saints. Well shall it be for him who at that sorrowful time shall be pleasing to God!

There the bodies which are free from iniquity shall go glad of soul, and the spirits shall resort to their bony 520 tenements, when the conflagration mounts to the skies. The dreadful flame shall be hot for many a one, when, sorely afraid, every soul, righteous or sinful, shall with its body go from its grave in the earth unto the judgment of God. The fire shall be astir, and shall consume iniquities.

There the righteous, after their period of exile, shall be enringed with their own deeds, the works they have wrought; these are the noble and winsome plants with 530 which the wild bird surrounds his own nest, so that it

suddenly vanishes in flame, shrivels under the sun, and
himself with it, thence receiving life anew after the
burning is overpast.   In like manner every one of
human kind invested with flesh shall be once more
young and comely, if so be he bring it to pass of his
own choice that the mighty King of glory is gracious
unto him in that assembly.   Then those holy spirits shall
chant aloud ; the righteous souls, pure and elect, shall 540
raise a song, voice after voice lauding the majesty of
their King ; they shall mount to glory with the rich
incense of their good deeds.   The spirits of men shall
be cleansed, brightly purified by the burning of fire.

11. THE TESTIMONY OF JOB

Let no one of mankind imagine that I compose my
song of lying words, writing it with poetic skill.   Hear
a prophecy, the utterances of Job.   Inspired in heart
by the Spirit, gloriously distinguished, he discoursed 550
boldly, and spake these words [1] :

' I scorn not in the thoughts of my heart, as a man
weary in body, to choose my deathbed in my nest, to
go hence on my long journey abject, overlaid with dust,
lamenting my former deeds, into the lap of earth ; for,
like the Phœnix, I shall after death, through the Lord's
grace, have new life after the resurrection, shall possess
joys with the Lord, where the illustrious band praise 560
the Beloved.   Never need I expect an end to that life,
that light, and those joys.   Though my body decay in
its earthy dwelling, a prey to worms, yet the God of

[1] Job 29. 18; 19. 25, 26.

hosts will release my soul after the period of dissolution, and awaken it to glory ; hope of this is never lack-
ing in my heart, for I have abiding and settled joy in
the Lord of angels.'

570   Thus the wise man, discerning of soul, the prophet
of God, sang in ancient days of his resurrection to life
eternal, that we might the better understand the glorious
sense which the famous bird signifies by his burning.

12. THE REUNION OF SOUL AND BODY

The bird gathers up the residue of the bones after the
fire, the ashes and embers, and carries them with his
feet toward the sun, to the courts of the Lord ; there,
580 with youth wholly renewed, restored in growth, he lives
for many years, in the land where none can threaten
with injury.   In this manner, by the power of the Lord,
shall souls journey with their bodies after death, like to
that bird, and, richly garnished with precious spicery,
shall pass to that blessedness where, fair above the hosts
in the City of glory, shines the Sun of righteousness.

13. THE JOYS OF THE BLESSED[1]

590   When, high above all heights, Christ the Savior shines
upon the righteous souls, there follow Him brilliant birds,
splendidly regenerated, spirits elect unto all eternity,
blissful exulting in that joyous home.   There the malicious, hostile fiend cannot harm them with his wiles, but
they live appareled with light in the peace of God,

[1] Cf. pp. 91–2, 136–7.

beauteous in glory, like unto the Phœnix. Each one's work shines bright in that joyous home before the face of the eternal Lord, in bliss unending, like to the sun. 600

There the beaming crown of each blessèd one, wondrously set with precious stones, towers above his head; their brows gleam, invested with splendor; the rare diadem of their Lord adorns every saint with light in that life where there is never abatement of the enduring joy, eternal and ever young; they live in beauty, gloriously arrayed in fair adornments, with the Father of the angels. 610

In that abode there is no grief for them — neither misfortune, nor poverty, nor days of toil, nor consuming hunger, nor fierce thirst, nor misery, nor age; the noble King bestows upon them every good. There the throng of spirits magnify the Savior and celebrate the might of heaven's King, singing praises to God. That band of kinsfolk makes melody sweet and clear about God's holy throne. With one voice of gladness saints and angels adore the peerless King: 620

'Peace, and wisdom, and blessing for these thy gifts, and for every good, be unto Thee, the true God, throned in majesty. Infinite, high, and holy is the power of thy might. The heavens, on high with the angels, are full of the glory, O Father almighty, Lord of all lords, and the earth also. Defend us, Author of creation. Thou art the Father almighty in the highest, the Lord of heaven.[1]' 630

---

[1] Cf. Rev. 7. 12; *Te Deum* (Isa. 6. 3); Mt. 21. 9 (?); and Cook's notes on *Chr.* 401 ff.

Thus the workers of righteousness, purified from evil, cry aloud in the glorious City, and proclaim His majesty. The multitude of the righteous chant in heaven their Emperor's praise :

'To Him alone is honor without end. Never was there a beginning of Him, an origin to His bliss. Though He
640 was born as a child into the world, yet the fulness of His holy power, His imperishable glory, still dwelt high above the heavens. Though He was to suffer the agony of death, a terrible torture, upon the rood-tree, yet the third day after the destruction of His body He regained his life by the Father's aid. So the Phœnix, young in his home, typifies the power of the Divine Child when he rises again from his ashes into the life of life, perfect in his
650 limbs. Just as the Savior brought us succor, life without end, by the death of His body, so this bird fills his two wings with sweet and delicious herbs, the beautiful produce of the earth, when he is ready to depart.'

14. EPILOGUE

These are the words (as books tell us), the utterances of saints whose soul is intent upon heaven, the gentle God, the joy of joys ; there they bring, as a gift to God the Lord, the ravishing fragrance of their words and
660 works into that glorious existence, into that radiant life. Blessing, and glory, and honor, and power be to Him ever, world without end, in the kingdom of heaven above ![1] He is rightful King of the world and of the heavenly host, invested with glory in the City beautiful.

[1] Cf. Rev. 5. 13.

The Author of light has granted to us that we may here obtain by our good deeds the joys of heaven. There we may visit the chiefest of kingdoms and sit on lofty thrones, live in an ecstasy of light and peace, possess abodes of bountiful gladness, enjoy days of prosperity, behold eternally the benign and gracious Lord of victory, and, blessèd with the angels, hymn His praise in songs that never end. Alleluia.

670

ALBERT S. COOK.

VII

CHARMS

The *Charms* are among the oldest extant specimens of English prose and verse, and in their first form were of heathen origin. Traces of early Germanic mythology (sometimes unintelligible) are therefore common. Some of the incantations remain practically unaffected by Christianity; others, such as the first and last here given, are in truth prayers, modern parallels to which (such as the blessing of the fields at Rogation-tide) may easily be discovered. Whether they be examined as survivals of an earlier stage of civilization, or as examples of the way in which the Christian church received and transformed the folk-lore of the people, they are of singular interest to the student of English origins; cf. Brooke, *English Literature from the Beginning to the Norman Conquest*, pp. 42–46.

A scholarly and interesting account of the charms, discussing all their chief aspects, may be found in the *Journal of American Folk-Lore* **22** 84, for April–June, 1909, in an article by Felix Grendon, entitled 'The Anglo-Saxon Charms.'

The following charms are all contained in the Grein-Wülker *Bibliothek der Angelsächsischen Poesie* **1** 312 ff.

CHARM FOR BEWITCHED LAND

Here is the remedy with which thou canst improve thy fields if they will not bring forth, or if any evil thing is done *to them* through sorcery or witchcraft.

At night, before daybreak, take four sods from the
four corners of the land, and mark how they had stood.
Next take oil, honey, and yeast, and milk of every sort
of cattle that is on that land, and a piece of every kind
of tree that is grown on that land except hard wood,
and a piece of every kind of herb whose name is known,
excepting only burdock.   Put holy water on *these*, and
then drip of it thrice on the base of the turfs, and say 10
these words : *Crescite*, grow, *et multiplicamini*, and
multiply, *et replete*, and fill, *terram*, this earth, *in
nomine Patris et Filii et Spiritus Sancti sint benedicti ;*
and *Pater noster* as often as the other *formula*.

After this take the sods to church, and let the priest
chant four masses over them, and have them turned with
the green side toward the altar.   Then bring them back
before sunset to where they were formerly.   Next make
four crosses of aspen, and write on each end *Matheus*
and *Marcus* and *Lucas* and *Johannes*.   Place a cross on
the bottom of each hole, and say : *Crux Matheus, crux
Marcus, crux Lucas, crux sanctus Johannes*.   Then take 20
the sods and lay them on top, and say the *Crescite* nine
times, and *Pater noster* as often.   Turn thyself then
toward the east, bow humbly, and say these words :

> I stand towards the east, for blessing I pray,
> I pray the God of glory, I pray the great Lord,
> I pray the holy Ruler of the realm of heaven,
> The earth I pray and heaven above,
> The true saint Mary,
> And the power of heaven and its high hall,   30
> That with the grace of God I may disclose
> This spell with my teeth ; *that* with steadfast thought
> *I may* generate the harvests for our temporal benefit,

Fill these fields with firm belief
And glorify these meadow-turfs ; for the prophet said
That he had grace in earthly kingdom
Who wisely gave alms according to the will of the Lord.

Then turn thrice following the course of the sun, stretch
thyself prostrate, and count there the litanies.   Say also
40 the *Tersanctus* to the end, and then chant *Benedicite* with
outstretched arms, and *Magnificat* and *Pater Noster*
thrice, and commend *thy prayer* to the praise and glory of
Christ, and St. Mary, and the Holy Rood, the angel that
guards the land, and all those that are subject to him.
When all that has been done, get some unknown seed
from beggars, and give them twice as much as thou takest
from them.   Then gather all thy plowing tackle together,
bore a hole in the beam, *and put therein* incense, and
fennel, and consecrated soap, and consecrated salt.   Take
the seed, and put it on the body of the plow, and then say:

Erce, Erce, Erce, mother of Earth,
50   May the Almighty, the eternal Lord, grant thee
Fields fertile and flourishing,
Fruitful and full of vigor,
.   .   .   bright harvests,
And the harvests of the broad barley,
Harvests of the white wheat,
And all the harvests of the earth.
O Eternal Lord, and His saints that are in heaven,
Grant to the *owner*
That his field be kept from every foe,
60   And defended against all harm,
From sorceries sown throughout the land.
Now I pray the King who created this world
That no garrulous woman or crafty man
Be able to pervert words thus spoken.

Then drive forth the plow, and cut the first furrow,
and say:

> Well be it with thee, Earth the mother of men!
> Fruitful mayest thou be in the embrace of God,
> Filled with food for the service of men.

Then take meal of every sort, and bake a loaf as 70
broad as will lie on the two hands, kneading it with milk
and with holy water, and lay it under the first furrow.
Say then:

> Full be the field with food for mankind,
> Bright in its blossoming; blessed be thou
> By the holy name of Him who shaped this heaven
> And this earth in which we live;
> May the God who made these grounds grant us growing gifts,
> That every kernel may come to use.

Then say thrice, *Crescite . . . in nomine Patris . . .*
sint benedicti, Amen; and *Pater noster* thrice.   80

CHARM FOR SWARMING BEES

Take earth, throw it up with thy right hand *from*
under thy right foot, and say:

> I take under foot, I have found it.
> Verily earth avails against every creature,
> And against mischief and mindlessness,
> And against the great tongue of man.

Throw dust over them when they swarm, and say:

> Sit ye, victor-dames, sink to earth,
> Never to fly wild to the wood!
> Be as mindful of my good   10
> As every man is of food and estate.

CHARM FOR A SUDDEN STITCH

Feverfew, and the red nettle that grows in through the house, and plantain ; seethe in butter.

Loud were they, lo loud, when over the hill they rode,
Resolute were they when over the land they rode ;
Now shield thyself, that thou mayest survive this malice !
Out, little spear, if herein it be !
   I stood under linden, under the light shield,
Where the mighty women mustered their force,
And whizzing spears they sent ;
10 I will send them back another,
A flying dart directly against them.
Out, little spear, if herein it be !
   The smith sat, he forged a little knife,
Smitten with the [1] iron heavily,
Out, little spear, if herein it be !
   Six smiths sat, war-spears they wrought,
Out, spear, not in, spear !
   If herein there be a bit of iron,
The work of witches, it shall melt !
20 If thou wert shot in the skin, or wert shot in the flesh,
Or wert shot in the blood,
Or wert shot in the limb, never may thy life be harmed !
If it were a shot of gods, or if it were a shot of elves,
Or if it were a shot of witches, now will I help thee.
This to thee as a remedy for the shot of gods, this to thee as a
   remedy for the shot of elves,
This to thee as a remedy for the shot of witches ; I will help
   thee.
Flee to the mountain-head ! [1]
Be thou whole, the Lord help thee !

Then take the knife, and put it into the liquid.

[1] MS. corrupt.

NINE HERBS CHARM

Remember, Wormwood, what thou didst reveal,
What thou didst prepare at the great proclamation.
'Una' thou art named, the eldest of herbs;
Thou art strong against three and against thirty,
Thou art strong against venom and against infection,
Thou art strong against the Evil Thing that goes throughout the land.
   And thou, Plantain, mother of herbs,
Open from the east, mighty within.
Over thee carts creaked, queens rode over thee,
Over thee brides made cries, bulls gnashed over thee.   10
All those thou didst withstand, and dashed against them;
So mayst thou withstand venom and infection
And the Evil Thing that goes throughout the land.
   Water-cress is this herb named; it grew on stone.
It stands against venom, it fights against pain.
   Nettle is this called; it dashes against venom,
It drives away cruel things, it casts out venom.
This is the herb that fought with the snake;
This is strong against venom, this is strong against infection,
This is strong against the Evil Thing that goes throughout the 20
   land.
   Fly now, Betonica, the less from the greater,
The greater from the less, till there be to them a cure for both.
   Remember, Camomile, what thou didst make known,
What thou didst bring to pass at Alorford,
That for the flying ill he never yielded up his life
After one prepared Camomile for him to eat.
   This is the herb that is called Wild-Apple.
The seal sent this over the back of the sea,
To heal the hurt of other venom.
These nine attacked nine venoms.   30
A serpent came sneaking; he slew a man.
Then took Woden nine glory-twigs,

Smote the serpent then so that it flew in nine pieces;
There the apple ended it and its venom,
So that it never would enter house again.
   Thyme and Fennel, two exceeding mighty ones,
These herbs the wise Lord made,
Holy in the heavens; He let them down,
40 Placed them, and sent them into the seven worlds
As a cure for all, the poor and the rich.
It stands against pain, it dashes against venom,
It is strong against three and against thirty,
Against the hand of an enemy and against the hand of the cursèd,
. . . And against the bewitching of my creatures.

   Now these nine herbs are strong against nine cursèd
things, against nine venoms and against nine infections:
against the red venom, against the gray venom, against
the white venom, against the blue venom, against the
50 yellow venom, against the green venom, against the black
venom, against the brown venom, against the purple
venom; against snake-blister, against water-blister, against
thorn-blister, against thistle-blister, against ice-blister,
against poison-blister; if any venom come flying from
the east, or if any come from the north, or any from the
west over the people.
   Christ stood over venom of every kind.   I alone know
running water, and the nine serpents behold it.   All
grasses may spring up with herbs, the sea vanish away,
all the salt water, when I blow this venom from thee.

CHARM FOR REGAINING LOST CATTLE

As soon as one says that thy cattle are lost, say first before thou say anything else :

> Bethlehem was named the town where Christ was born ;
> It is renowned through all the world ;
> So may this deed become famed among men
> Through the Holy Rood of Christ.   Amen.

Then pray thrice toward the east, and say thrice : *Crux Christi ab oriente reducat;* then pray thrice toward the west, and say thrice : *Crux Christi ab occidente reducat;* then pray thrice toward the south, and say thrice : *Crux Christi ab austro reducat;* then pray thrice toward the north, and say thrice : *Crux Christi ab aquilone reducat.   Crux Christi abscondita est et inventa est.*   The Jews crucified Christ, they did the worst of deeds, they hid that which they could not hide, so may this deed in no wise be hidden, through the Holy Rood of Christ. Amen.

WILLIAM O. STEVENS.

BIBLIOGRAPHY

REFERENCES FOR STUDENTS OF OLD ENGLISH
POETRY

NOTE. — So great has been the progress of Old English scholarship in the past few years that none of the following books presents the latest and most reliable views on such points as date, source, authorship, etc. Discussion of these topics must be sought in critical editions of the poems, and in the scholarly journals. The editors have tried to supply references to these in the prefatory notes. A fuller bibliography of important works will be found in Cook's *First Book in Old English*, 3d ed. (Boston, Ginn and Company), pp. 235–244.

ALOIS BRANDL, 'Englische Literatur,' pp. 941–1134 of Paul's *Grundriss der Germanischen Philologie*, 2d ed., Vol. 2, Part 1, Strassburg, 1909.
> The most scholarly treatment of the subject.

BERNHARD TEN BRINK, *Early English Literature*, translated by H. M. Kennedy, New York, 1883, pp. 1–115.
> A good general account, which, though old, has never been wholly superseded.

STOPFORD BROOKE, *The History of Early English Literature*, New York (Macmillan), 1892.

———— ———— *English Literature from the Beginning to the Norman Conquest*, New York (Macmillan), 1898.
> Often fanciful, and in general not authoritative. The earlier volume is fuller, but the later contains some material not in the first.

Cambridge History of English Literature, Vol. 1, 'From the Beginnings to the Cycles of Romance,' pp. 1–71.
> Lacking thoroughness, and even, at times, reliability.

W. P. KER, *English Literature : Mediæval*, London and New York, 1912.
> Of value to the student of literary relations.

GUSTAV KÖRTING, *Grundriss der Geschichte der Englischen Litteratur*, 3d ed., Münster, 1899, pp. 9–70.
> Bibliographical references.

E. LEGOUIS and L. CAZAMIAN, *Histoire de la Littérature Anglaise*, Paris, 1924 (also appearing in English), pp. 3–54.
> A literary estimate comparatively free from British and German influence.

HENRY MORLEY, *English Writers*, New York (Cassell), 1887
> Vols. 1 and 2 cover the Old English period. Often lacks independence.

HENRY SWEET, 'Sketch of the History of Anglo-Saxon Poetry,' in Hazlitt's edition of Warton's *History of English Poetry*, London, 1871.
> Gives in a few pages an excellent notion of the *scope* of Old English literature.

R. P. WÜLKER, *Grundriss zur Geschichte der Angelsächsischen Litteratur*, Leipzig, 1885.
> Full bibliographical references to date of publication. It should be supplemented by the use of Körting's *Grundriss* (see above).

APPENDIX I

SELECTIONS FROM THE VERSE-TRANSLATIONS OF BEOWULF

The following selections are gathered here in order to facilitate comparison of the various media which have been used in translating Old English.

A critical account of all existing translations of *Beowulf*, together with extracts, may be found in Tinker's bibliography, *The Translations of Beowulf*, New York (Holt), 1902, *Yale Studies in English* XVI.

[*The Death of Beowulf*, vv. 2813-2820]

Wackerbarth's Translation

'Thou art the last remaining Stay
    Of our Wægmunding Stem,
My Sons hath Fate swept all away,
Earls in their Might, to Death's dark Sway;
    And I must after them.'
This ere the Pyre the old Man chose,
The Battle-wave that furious glows,
    His bosom's latest Word.
And from his Breast his Spirit goes
To seek the blessed Doom of those
    Who ne'er from Truth have err'd.   1849.

J. Lesslie Hall's Translation

'Thou art latest left of the line of our kindred,
Of Wægmunding people: Weird hath offcarried
All of my kinsmen to the Creator's glory,

175

Earls in their vigor : I shall after them fare.'
'Twas the agèd liegelord's last-spoken word in
His musings of spirit, ere he mounted the fire,
The battle-waves burning: from his bosom departed
His soul to seek the sainted ones' glory.

1892.

Lumsden's Translation

'Alone thou'rt left, the last

Of all our Wægmund race ; my kinsmen, earls of might, have
    passed,
Weird-driv'n, to doom ; and thither too I go.'

Of his heart's thought

'Twas the last word the old man spake ere he the bale-fire
    sought, —
The hotly raging waves of flame ; and from its dwelling fared
His spirit forth to seek the doom for righteous men prepared.

1881.

Garnett's Translation

'Thou art the last left of our own kindred
Of the Wægmundings.   Weird carried away all
Of mine own kinsmen at the time appointed,
Earls in their strength : I shall go after them.'
That was to the agéd the very last word
In his breast-thoughts, ere the pyre he chose,
The hot fiery waves : from his breast went
His soul to seek the doom of the saints.

1882.

Morris and Wyatt's Translation

'Thou art the end-leaving of all of our kindred,
The Wægmundings ; Weird now hath swept all away
Of my kinsmen, and unto the Doom of the Maker
The earls in their might ; now after them shall I.'
That was to the aged lord youngest of words

Of his breast-thoughts, ere ever he chose him the bale,
The hot battle-wellings; from his heart now departed
His soul, to seek out the doom of the soothfast.

1895.

Longfellow translated a few extracts in his *Poets and Poetry of Europe*, of which the following may serve as a specimen:

[Beowulf's Sea-Voyage, vv. 217–224 a]

Then went over the sea-waves,
Hurried by the wind,
The ship with foamy neck,
Most like a sea-fowl,
Till about one hour
Of the second day
The curved prow
Had passed onward
So that the sailors
The land saw,
The shore-cliffs shining,
Mountains steep,
And broad sea-noses.
Then was the sea-sailing
Of the Earl at an end.

1838.

APPENDIX II

THE SONG OF BRUNANBURH

For this translation see Tennyson's note on p. 25. A comparison of this version with the poetical one will be instructive.

Athelstan King, lord of earls, giver of costly gifts among barons, and his brother Edmund Atheling — lifelong glory they gain'd in the strife by Brunanburh with the edges of their swords. They clove the wall of shields; they hew'd the battle-shields of lindenwood; with hammer'd brands they hew'd them — these sons of Edward.

This was their nobleness from those that went before them, that they, so often, in combat against every foeman, should guard their land, their hoards, and their homes.

The spoilers cringed; the Scottishmen crouch'd; and the ship-crews fell: they were doom'd to the death; the field flow'd with blood of warriors, from when the sun on high, the mighty star in the morning-tide, the bright lamp of God the everlasting Lord, glided over earth, even until this noble creature sank to his setting.

There lay stricken down by the spear many warrior-men of the North, — shot over the shield; many a Scotsman also, full-wearied with war. All day long the West Saxons, — their chosen men in companies, — follow'd on the track the race of their loathing; quickly they hack'd at the fliers from behind — with swords sharpen'd by the grindstone. The Mercians stinted not their hard hand-play among those heroes, that along with Anlaf, over the weltering waves, in the bark's bosom, had made for the land. In fight they were doom'd to the death. There lay five young kings, sword-silenced on the war-field: there lay seven earls of Anlaf — and ravagers innumerable — sea-men and Scotsmen.

The Norse leader was hunted away; needs must he fly to the stem of his ship, — few of his own were with him: the keel drave afloat; the king fled forth; on the fallow flood he saved his life. There came likewise in flight to his kith in the North the wary Constantinus, the hoary warrior.

No need had he to boast of the welcome of swords; he was forlorn of his kin, he was forlorn of his friends, they were fell'd on that throng'd field, slain in the strife; and he left his son upon the place of slaughter, wounds had gash'd him into pieces, he was yet young in war.

No need had he to vaunt of the carnage of axes, that white-hair'd Baron! that aged Traitor! nor had he, nor any more had Anlaf, with the ruin of their armies, aught of reason for laughter, as though they were better in the works of war, in the struggle of standards on the battle-ground, in the meeting of men at the gathering of spears, in the wrestling of weapons, where-withal they had play'd on the field of slaughter against the sons of Edward.

Then past forth a red remnant of the javelins, the Northmen in their nailed barks, on the sounding sea, over the deep water, to make for Dyflen, for Ireland again — they were shamed in their souls. But the brothers, the king, and the Atheling, both together, sought their kith *in* the land of the West Saxon, rejoicing in battle.

Many a carcase they left behind them, many a sallow skin for the swarthy raven with horny beak to tear; the livid corpse they left behind them for the ern with white tail to gorge as carrion, for the greedy war-hawk, and for that gray beast, the wolf of the weald.

Never before in this island was a huger slaughter of men fell'd by the sword-edge (among those of which the books tell us, the ancient chroniclers) — never before — since the Angles and Saxons came up hither from the East, and over the broad brine sought Britain; when haughty war-smiths overcame the Welsh-men, and earls full of the lust of glory gat hold of the land.

HALLAM TENNYSON.

APPENDIX III

BEDE'S ACCOUNT OF THE POET CÆDMON

This account, taken from Bede's *Ecclesiastical History of the English People*, Book 4, chapter 24, is absolutely everything that we know of Cædmon, save for the original text of the verses paraphrased below and known as *Cædmon's Hymn* (see p. 76). According to Henry Bradley (*Encyc. Brit.*, 11th ed. 4 935), the name 'Cædmon' probably = British 'Cadman,' Old Celtic 'Catumanus,' where the first element signifies 'war.'

There was in the monastery of this abbess a certain brother especially distinguished by the grace of God, since he was wont to make poems breathing of piety and religion. Whatever he learned of Sacred Scripture by the mouth of interpreters, he in a little time gave forth in poetical language composed with the greatest sweetness and depth of feeling, in English, his native tongue; and the effect of his poems was ever and anon to incite the souls of many to despise the world and long for the heavenly life. Not but that there were others after him among the people of the Angles who sought to compose religious poetry; but none there was who could equal him, for he did not learn the art of song from men, nor through the means of any man; rather did he receive it as a free gift from God. Hence it came to pass that he never was able to compose poetry of a frivolous or idle sort; none but such as pertain to religion suited a tongue so religious as his. Living always the life of a layman until well advanced in years, he had never learned the least thing about poetry. In fact, so little did he understand of it that when at a feast it would be ruled that every one present should, for the entertainment of the others, sing in turn, he would, as soon as he saw the harp coming anywhere near him, jump up from the table in the midst of the banqueting, leave the place, and make the best of his way home.

This he had done at a certain time, and, leaving the house where the feast was in progress, had gone out to the stable where the care of the cattle had been assigned to him for that night. There, when it was time to go to sleep, he had lain down for that purpose. But while he slept some one stood by him in a dream, greeted him, called him by name, and said, ' Cædmon, sing me something.' To this he replied, ' I know not how to sing, and that is the very reason why I left a feast and came here, because I could not sing.' But the one who was talking with him answered, ' No matter, you are to sing for me.' ' Well, then,' said he, ' what is it that I must sing? ' ' Sing,' said the other, ' the beginning of created things.' At this reply he immediately began to sing verses in praise of God the Creator, verses that he had never heard, and whose meaning is as follows: ' Now should we praise the Keeper of the heavenly kingdom, the might of the Creator and His counsel, the works of the Father of glory; how He, though God eternal, became the Author of all marvels. He, the almighty Guardian of mankind, first created for the sons of men heaven as a roof, and afterwards the earth.' This is the meaning, but not the precise order, of the words which he sang in his sleep; for no songs, however well they may be composed, can be rendered from one language into another without loss of grace and dignity. When he rose from sleep, he remembered all that he had sung while in that state, and shortly after added, in the same strain, many more words of a hymn befitting the majesty of God.

In the morning he went to the steward who was set over him, and showed him what gift he had acquired. Being led to the abbess, he was bidden to make known his dream and repeat his poem to the many learned men who were present, that they all might give their judgment concerning the thing which he related, and whence it was; and they were unanimously of the opinion that heavenly grace had been bestowed upon him by the Lord. They then set about expounding to him a piece of sacred history or teaching, bidding him, if he could, to turn it into the rhythm of poetry. This he undertook to do, and departed. In the morning he returned and delivered the passage assigned to him, converted into an excellent poem. The abbess, honoring the grace of God as displayed in the man, shortly afterward instructed him to forsake the condition of a layman and take upon himself the vows of a monk. She thereupon received him into the monastery with his whole family, and made him one of the company of the brethren, commanding that he should be taught the whole course and succession of Biblical history. He, in turn, calling to mind what he was able to learn by the hearing of the ear, and, as it were, like a clean animal, chewing upon it as a cud, transformed it all into most agreeable poetry; and, by echoing it back in a more harmonious form, made his teachers in turn listen to him. Thus he rehearsed the creation of the world, the origin of man, and all the story of Genesis; the departure of Israel from Egypt and their entry into the Promised Land, together with many other histories from Holy Writ; the incarnation of our Lord, his passion, resurrection, and ascension into heaven; the coming of the Holy Ghost and the teaching of the Apostles; moreover, he made many poems about the terror of the future judgment, the awfulness of the pains of hell, and the joy of the heavenly kingdom, besides a great number about the mercies and judgments of God. In all these he exerted himself to allure men from the love of wickedness, and to impel them to the love and practice of righteous living; for he was a very devout man, humbly submissive to the monastic rule, but full of consuming zeal against those who were disposed to act otherwise.

Hence it came to pass that he ended his life with a fair death. For when the hour of his departure drew nigh, he was afflicted for the space of a fortnight with a bodily weakness which seemed to prepare the way; yet it was so far from severe that he was able during the whole of that time to walk about and converse. Near at hand there was a cottage, to which those who were sick and appeared nigh unto death were usually taken. At the approach of evening on the same night when he was to leave the world, he desired his attendant to make ready a place there for him to take his rest. The attendant did so, though he could not help wondering at the request, since he did not seem in the least like a person about to die. When he was placed in the infirmary, he was some-how full of good humor, and kept talking and joking with those who had already been brought there. Some time after midnight he asked whether they had the Eucharist at hand. 'What do you need of the Eucharist?' they answered, 'you are n't going to die yet, for you are just as full of fun in talking with us as if nothing were the matter with you.' 'Never mind,' said he, 'bring me the Eucharist.' Taking it in his hand, he asked, 'Are you all at peace with me, and free from any grudge or ill-will?' 'Yes,' they all responded, 'we are perfectly at peace with you, and cherish no grievance whatever.' 'But are you,' said they, 'entirely at peace with us?' 'Yes, my dear children,' he answered without hesitation, 'I am at peace with all the servants of God.' And thus saying, he made ready for his entrance into the other life by partaking of the heavenly journey-bread. Not long after he inquired, 'How near is it to the hour when the brethren are wakened for lauds?' 'But a little while,' was the reply. 'Well then,' said he, 'let us wait for that hour,' and, making over himself the sign of the cross, he laid his head on the pillow, and falling into a light slumber, ended his life in silence. And so it came to pass that, as he had served the Lord in simplicity and purity of mind, and with serene attachment and loyalty, so by a serene death he left the world, and went to look upon His face. And meet in truth it was that the tongue which had indited so many helpful words in praise of the Creator, should frame its very last words in His praise, while in the act of signing himself with the cross, and of commending his spirit into His hands. And that he foresaw his death is apparent from what has here been related.

ALBERT S. COOK.

APPENDIX IV

FRAGMENT I OF THE OLD SAXON GENESIS[1]

(Cf. note on pp. 104-5)

'Uuela that thu nu, Eua, habas,' quad Aðam, 'ubilo gimarakot
unkaro selbaro sīð! Nu maht thu sean thia suarton hell
ginon grādaga; nu thu sia grimman maht
hinana gihōrean; nis heðanrīki
gelīhc sulicaro lōgnun; thit uuas alloro lando scōniust,
that uuit hier thuruh unkas Herran thank hebbian muostun,
thar thu them ni hōrdis thie unk thesan haram giried,
that uuit Uualdandas uuord farbrākun,
Heðankuningas. Nu uuit hriuuig mugun
10 sorogon for them sīða, uuand he hunk selbo gibood
that uuit hunk sulic uuīti uuardon scoldin
haramo mēstan. Nu thuingit mi giū hungar endi thurst,
bitter balouuerk,[2] thero uuāron uuit ēr bēðero tuom.
Hū sculun uuit nu libbian, efto hū sculan uuit an thesum liahta[3] uuesan,
nu hier huuīlum uuind kumit uuestan efto ōstan,
sūðan efto nordan, gisuuerek upp drībit.
Kumit haglas skion himile bitengi,
ferið ford an gimang, that is firinum kald;
huīlum thanne fan himile hēto skīnit,
20 blīkit thiu berahto sunna; uuit hier thus bāra standat,
unnuuerid mið giuuādi. Nis unk hier uuiht biuoran
ni te skadoua ni[4] te scūra; unk nis hier scattas uuiht
te meti gimarcot; uuit hebbiat unk giduan mahtigna God,
Uualdand, uurēðan. Te hui sculun uuit uuerðan nu?
Nu mag mi that hreuuan, that ik is io bad heðanrīkean God,
Uualdand al . . .

---

[1] From Piper, *Die Altsächsische Bibeldichtung*, pp. 437-9.
[2] MS. balouuerek.   [3] MS. liatha.
[4] The beginning of this line uncertain in the MS.

OLD ENGLISH GENESIS 790–820

Adam gemǣlde and tō Euan sprǣc: 790
‘ Hwæt, þū, Eue, hæfst yfele gemearcod
uncer sylfra sīð. Gesyhst þū nū þā sweartan helle,
grǣdige and gīfre? Nū þū hīe grimman meaht
heonane gehȳran. Nis heofenrīce
gelīc þām līge, ac þis is landa betst,
þæt wit þurh uncres Hearran [1] þanc habban mōston,
þǣr þū þām ne hīerde þe unc þisne hearm gerǣd,
þæt wit Waldendes word forbrǣcon,
Heofoncyninges. Nū wit hrēowige magon
sorglan for þis sīðe, forþon hē unc self bebēad   800
þæt wit unc wīte warian sceolden,
hearma mǣstne. Nū slīt me hunger and þurst
bitre on brēostum, þæs wit bēgra ǣr
wǣron orsorge on ealle tīd.
Hū sculon wit nū libban, oððe on þȳs lande wesan,
gif hēr wind cymð westan oððe ēastan,
sūðan oððe norðan, gesweorc ūpfǣreð?
Cymeð hægles scūr hefone getenge,
fǣreð forst ongemang, se byð fyrnum ceald;
hwīlum of heofnum hāte scīneð,   810
blīcð þēos beorhte sunne, and wit hēr baru standað,
unwered wǣdo. Nys unc wuht beforan
tō scūrsceade, nē sceattes wiht
tō mete gemearcod, ac unc is mihtig God,
Waldend, wrāðmōd. Tō hwon sculon wit weorðan nū?
Nu mē mæg hrēowan þæt ic bæd heofnes God,
Waldend [þone gōdan, þæt hē þē hēr worhte tō mē
of liðum mīnum, nū þū mē forlǣred hæfst
on mīnes Herran hete; swā mē nū hrēowan mæg
ǣfre tō aldre, þæt ic þē mīnum ēagum geseah.’]   820

---

[1] Kluge thinks (*Etymologische Wörterbuch der Deutschen Sprache*, s.v. Herr)
that the Low German word (see the Old Saxon form) probably entered England
in the ninth century as *hearra* (see also line 819), and later reached Scandinavia.

INDEX OF SUBJECTS

INDEX OF MEDIA

INDEX OF TITLES